Destiny of Discipleship

15 Lessons you need to learn to fulfill God's plan for your life

Written by Eric Foster

Destiny of Discipleship

15 Lessons you need to learn to fulfill God's plan for your life

Written by Eric Foster

All Bible quotations, unless otherwise indicated, are taken from the *Holy Bible, New International Version* (NIV). Copyright © 1973, 1978, 1984 by International Bible Society. Used by permission of Zondervan. All rights reserved.

Scriptures marked "NKJV" are taken from the, *New King James Version*. Copyright © 1982 by Thomas Nelson, Inc. Used by permission. All rights reserved.

Scriptures marked "KJV" are taken from the *Holy Bible, King James Version.*

Scriptures marked "NASB" are taken from the New American Standard Bible, © Copyright 1960, 1962, 1963, 1968, 1971, 1972, 1973, 1975, 1977 by The Lockman Foundation. Used by permission.

Destiny of Discipleship

ISBN 1-59919-013-3
Printed in the United States of America

Copyright © 2006 Eric Foster
Cover Design by Rebecca Robinson Copyright © 2006

Published By:
Elim Publishing
1679 Dalton Road
Lima, NY 14485

No part of this book may be reproduced or transmitted in any form or by any means, electronic or mechanical, including photocopying, recording, or by any information storage and retrieval system, without prior written permission from the publisher.

DEDICATION

To my wife, Allison – a precious gift from God
and a constant reminder of His goodness.
Thank you for your love and encouragement.

Contents

INTRODUCTION

Do we really need another book? Have you ever gone into a bookstore and noticed large empty spaces on the shelves and thought, “I wish somebody would write more books to fill up all the empty space.” I’m guessing that you haven’t. Most bookstore shelves are jammed with books on every topic, from art to zoology. So why write another book to be card cataloged and filed on a bookstore shelf? Isn’t it just going to eventually end up with all of last year’s best sellers, in a pile in the front of the store marked “75% off”?

My hope is that this book will share with you the truth about being a disciple of Jesus Christ. I want to challenge you to not only accept Him as Lord, but to truly follow Him, finding out His destiny for you. I want to give you the tools you need for living that out every day. Hopefully, this book will not be one that you read and then file on a bookshelf, or sell at a garage sale. I wrote this book for you to read, re-read and then give to someone you know who can benefit from it—a neighbor, a co-worker, or a friend. We all know people who are hurting, lost and searching for answers to life’s trials. Why not give them an opportunity to discover that the answer they have been looking for is right under their nose? God, the Creator of Heaven and Earth, has been quietly calling to them in the midst of their trouble, but they haven’t heard His call.

Maybe you are in that place right now—searching for a reason to go on, to move ahead with a life that seems hopeless. I assure you that it is not by accident that you are reading this. My hope is that as you read on and turn the pages in this book, your life, both physically and spiritually, will take a turn for the better; that your understanding of who God is, and what He is all about, will be drastically challenged. I hope that you will come away from this study with an understanding of your place in His family. Stop running from God and turn toward His love and compassion. He will not fail you. Truly knowing Him will strengthen every area of your life. Give Him a chance to prove His undying love to you, and you won't be disappointed.

You may have been a Christian for a while and have fallen into a rut in your spiritual walk. The fire that once burned brightly is now only a flicker, ready to be blown out at any moment. You can re-kindle the excitement for living as a disciple of Jesus Christ—a true disciple—one who follows His commands and leans on Him daily. You can overcome the complacency that has crept into your spiritual life and once again be filled with a passion for Him.

At the end of each section, take a few minutes to reflect on the questions asked. I encourage you to either keep a journal of your responses or simply write them down in the space provided. Writing your responses is critical to ensure that you will be able to see how you have grown through your study of God's plan for your life—your destiny of discipleship.

God bless you as you start this new chapter in your life!

CHAPTER 1
ARE WE REALLY INDEPENDENT?

Tim awoke to the familiar sound of his phone ringing from halfway across the room. He looked at the clock and saw it was 7:53 AM. *What day is it?* he wondered, as he flung the sheets off his bed and put his feet on the floor. As he stumbled across the floor, trying to adjust his eyes to the light pouring in from the window, he realized it was Friday. He picked up the phone and found his friend Jon on the other end.

"Tim!" he shouted. "You're gonna be late for our final!"

"Okay, okay, I'll be there in a minute," Tim replied and hung up the phone. *Finals – God help me!* he thought.

As Tim frantically got dressed, he recalled his night of celebration with his friends and how he had finally gotten to bed at 4:30 AM. *What was I thinking?* he thought, as he threw on a shirt that was in the pile on the floor and searched frantically for his jeans. *I am never going to do that again!* As he rushed to class, he tried to remember everything that he had learned that year in class. Had he studied enough? What if he didn't pass? What if he didn't graduate? What would he do? He stopped just outside the familiar tall brown brick building—Jefferson Hall. He had spent so many days there trying to learn just enough to get through the next test. He glanced at his watch. 8:04 AM. Not bad, he thought. He shook his head and went inside. He paused just outside the door to the lecture hall. "God," he said out loud, "if You're really out there, help me pass this, okay?" He paused and thought for a moment. "If You help me with this, I'll do whatever You want me to." He waited for a second as if he were expecting an audible answer and slowly pushed open the door.

How many of us have been in a similar situation? You may not be a college student, but how many times have you not prepared for a "test" in your life and turned to God at the last minute to rescue you from certain disaster? I think at some time we have all been in Tim's shoes. We have all had difficult situations to deal with: a relationship begins to fail, we lose a loved one, we lose a job suddenly. Why is it that so often we wait to call on God as though He is our "last hope"? It seems we would rather be in a tough situation by ourselves and be "independent" than rely on His power and strength that are available to us.

Why? Why do we think we are independent? We depend on others every day of our lives, all throughout the day, from when we wake up until our heads hit the pillow. We depend on the electricity to be there to run our alarm clocks, the water to be there for our morning shower, the bus driver, taxi or subway to be there to get us to where we are going. We depend on the grocery stores to have food on their shelves and the gas station to have gas at the pumps. We depend on our employer to compensate us for our time. When we drive, we depend on the drivers headed in the opposite direction to stay in their lane. We are a dependent people. So why do we feel so independent?

What is independence? Webster defines independence as: *not subject to control by others; not affiliated with a larger controlling unit; not requiring or relying on others.* Even though we may think we are independent, we are truly dependent on numerous people every day as we saw above. So why, in our culture, is dependence looked at as a negative? Maybe it's because when we hear that someone is dependent, it is usually in the context of relying on a "crutch" to get through the day, such as being drug-dependent, alcohol-dependent, or co-dependent in a relationship, etc. We rarely hear of "healthy" people being dependent on others. Because of this, we create in our minds a false perception that dependency is what happens when someone can't deal with life or can't handle a situation and must turn to an outside source to "bail them out."

We have been brought up in a "do-it-yourself" culture. We are expected to be able to handle anything that is thrown at us at a moment's notice. We focus so much on what we can or should be able to do, that it leaves very little time for us to reflect on things we cannot do. And when we find something that we can't do, we are only a few clicks of a mouse away from finding out how to do it on the Internet. Several years ago, if you wanted to put a small addition on your home or remodel your kitchen, you would call a contractor who specialized in that type of work. You would call an expert. Today, you can stop by a home improvement superstore and within a few minutes of browsing their massive aisles, you can be an "expert" in it yourself. It is almost as if we want to be able to handle anything so that we need no one. This attitude of "I don't need anyone" is destined for disaster. To live as a truly independent person—one who doesn't rely on anybody—we will need to move to a deserted island without electricity or running water, eating only what we catch from the ocean, and living in a house we made from scraps of wood. We will find ourselves alone on the seashore. This would bring us to a lonely place.

How did this all get started? Why are we such an independent-thinking people? It is nothing new. We were created to be completely dependent on God. He was to be our source for everything. We were created to worship and fellowship with Him in an intimate way. When mankind fell and sin entered the world, the entire order of God's system for us was disturbed. Our intimate fellowship was broken. We stopped being dependent on God and started relying on ourselves. Instead of God providing all of our needs and life being one of enjoyment, work became laborious and life became empty without Him. The only way to restore balance and to gain back our intimacy with God is through relationship with His Son, Jesus Christ.

The warmth of the summer sun bore down on Tim as he walked across the campus to Jefferson Hall. *This is the day of truth*, he thought to himself. He would either find out he had passed the most difficult exam of his college career and would graduate in a couple weeks, or he would have to take classes this summer to make up the credits.

He already had a job lined up to start in two weeks, as the assistant business manager in a local law firm. This was going to be his first "real job." What would he do if he failed? As he walked down the hallway toward the bulletin board outside the dean's office, his heart beat a little faster. He approached the board and scanned down the list of his classmates and found his name. 72. He passed! All of the pressure of the semester drained out of his shoulders as he saw his grade. He was finally done with college. He could start his career and his life.

Two weeks later, as he walked from his car to the door of his new job, the excitement of his new life was almost palpable. He opened the door, was greeted by the receptionist and ushered into his new office. For the next two weeks, he was busy settling in his office, attending meetings with the partners, and trying to remember all the new names and faces of the staff. The hours and days flew by.

Every morning on his walk from the parking lot to the front door, he passed a small church that seemed to always have something new going on. He noticed that the sign out front, which welcomed visitors, seemed to change daily with a new quote, joke, or comment. He began to look forward to seeing the new messages.

Many times he saw the man he believed to be the pastor out front. He was a friendly, middle-aged man with a beard who always seemed to be in a good mood. The man always waved and called, "Good morning, son!" as Tim passed by. Tim would wave politely and go on his way to work.

One morning as he passed by the sign, he stopped in his tracks. He couldn't quite explain it, but he had an eerie feeling as though the sign was meant for him alone. The words haunted him as he went about business that day. He couldn't get them out of his head. When he walked past them again that night, the haunting words pierced his heart. "God answers prayer. Are you willing to answer His call?" Suddenly he was reminded of the "silly" prayer he had prayed before his exam. It was as if somehow that friendly pastor knew that he had prayed that prayer. *It can't be*, he thought. *Tim, don't be ridiculous. It must be for somebody else.* He walked by, shaking his head.

The next morning he noticed the same eerie message. *Weird*, he thought. *I wonder when he is going to change his sign.* Tim glanced around for the nice man. He saw him behind the church. *Maybe he hasn't gotten to it yet*, he concluded. That night on his way past the church, he noticed it was still there. *That's unusual*, he thought. *I hope that guy is okay.* Almost two weeks went by and every day Tim glanced over at the sign, looking for a new message. But every morning he saw the same message, and now it was starting to wear on him. Why didn't he change his sign? Tim stopped in front of the sign and just stared. His mind drifted back to a sermon he once heard about being "called" by God to do something "religious" with your life. But that was years ago, and besides, this was the real world. That doesn't happen today—especially to him.

Suddenly he heard the door of the church being pushed open by the pastor. Tim turned around and said "Good morning."

The man came down the steps and walked toward Tim. "Hello there. Isn't it a glorious day? Do you hear the birds singing?" He looked up at the old oak tree, trying to spot some of the birds. "Isn't it soothing?"

"Yeah, it's a nice day," Tim replied.

The man smiled and said, "I'm Pastor Steve," as he extended his hand.

"Hi. I'm Tim. Tim Riley. It's nice to meet you."

"It's finally nice to meet you, too." Pastor Steve continued, "I see you walk by often. Do you work around here?"

Work! Tim had almost forgotten. He was going to be late. "Actually," he said, looking at his watch, "I'm going to be late for work. It was nice to meet you, Pastor Steve," and he headed down the street.

He got a few steps away and heard Pastor Steve say, "Come by for lunch today and we can talk about the sign." Tim stopped in his tracks. He turned around and looked at the man in disbelief.

He heard himself say, "I'll be here at 12:30," and he walked on.

That morning was a blur. *What is he going to talk to me about? Is he going to try to have me join his church? What was the sign all about?* Twelve o'clock came faster that day than any other day he could remember. As he picked up a few things on his desk and got ready to go to the church, fear overcame him. He began to sweat bullets. What would he talk to this guy about? He wasn't exactly the picture of a "church person." He had been down some roads that he was not about to share— especially with a pastor! And the sign. He kept thinking about the sign. He wandered down the tree-lined street and nervously climbed the steps to the door of the church. He opened the door, took a deep breath and went inside.

As he went in, he noticed that the sign had been changed. "Pancake breakfast this Sunday from 7-9 a.m." *What is that all about?* he wondered. He nervously walked down the hall and saw Pastor Steve in his office.

"Come in!" he called, as he stood up from his desk. Tim walked into his office.

"Hi. Is this a good time?" he asked, searching for something to say.

"It's a great time, Tim. Have a seat. Would you like a drink?"

Tim slowly sat down and began to feel at ease. "No, thank you. I'm fine."

"How was your morning?" Pastor Steve asked politely.

Tim thought and answered, "I think it was good. I can't really remember."

Pastor Steve smiled and continued, "I saw that you were admiring our sign out front."

"Yeah. Can I ask why you left it the same for so long?" Tim asked.

Pastor Steve smiled and said, "I'm not certain, but I hope to know by the end of our talk today."

Tim's heart began to race and his palms became sweaty. *What did he mean? Who is this guy?* "Excuse me?" he asked nervously.

"Well, Tim," started Pastor Steve, "about three weeks ago I got a feeling that I was supposed to put that message up. I didn't really know why, but I couldn't get that phrase out of my head. Sometimes God works like that. He won't leave me alone until I follow orders, you know?"

Tim thought, *I'm starting to*, but just nodded his head.

Pastor Steve went on, "So I put the sign up there and felt like God was telling me that it was staying there until He told me to take it down. I didn't know why. You can't imagine how many calls I've received from people all over town asking why it hasn't been changed! My doctor even called and asked if I was okay. It caused quite a stir in this small town!"

"But today," he continued, "when I saw you staring at the sign, I felt as though He was saying, 'This is why I had you put the sign up.'" Tim could feel his face get warm as the blood rushed into it. He couldn't believe what he was hearing, *Could this be true?* he wondered. "That's why I came out to meet you before you left this morning. I felt that I was supposed to talk to you. What does the message on the sign mean to you, Tim?"

"Well," Tim started, "it sounds crazy, but I think I made a pact with God or something. About two months ago, I told God that if He helped me pass my final, I would do whatever He wanted me to. And for the last week or so I haven't been able to think straight. All I can think about is your sign and that I'm supposed to do something for God. It's crazy!"

Pastor Steve smiled and said, "You're not crazy, Tim. Let me ask you a question. Do you know Jesus?" Tim thought that was a strange question.

"Sure, I know Jesus. Who doesn't know Him?"

"Okay, do you have a relationship with Him?" Pastor Steve proceeded.

Tim thought and answered sheepishly, "I guess so. I mean, what's the difference?"

"Well, do you know who the president is?"

"Of course I do," Tim exclaimed with confusion on his face.

"Okay, how often do you call him; or he you? What's his favorite color, what does he like on his pizza? You see, Tim, you may know *who* he is, but you don't know *him*, right? Well, it's the same with God. Millions of people are lost, without knowing God, but they know who He is. They think it's the same, but it's totally different. Jesus even said that you can cast out demons and heal the sick, yet never truly

> know Him. Mark 3:11 tells us that even the demons recognized Jesus as the Son of God. They knew *who* He was, but that's not enough. You need to know Him, personally. And that comes through inviting Him into your life as your Savior through faith, and accepting the free gift of salvation that He offers to you.
>
> "You see, God created man to be in relationship with Him; but because of sin, man was separated from Him. It is as if there is a great gulf between man and God. Religion and good works don't bridge the gap. There is only one way back to God. Jesus came, lived a perfect life, died in your place, and waits for you to invite Him into your life as Savior and Lord. He wants nothing more than for you to acknowledge His lordship, and to ask Him to come into your life, forgive your sins, give you a new start, and be the Lord of your life. Does that sound like what you want, Tim?"
>
> With tears in his eyes, Tim lowered his head and said, "Yes, that is exactly what I want."

If you know who Jesus is, but never took time to accept His gift of salvation by inviting Jesus into your life and making Him the true Lord of your life, you can do that now, just as Tim did. The one thing God desires to have more than anything else is for you to be in a right relationship with Him. So many people drift through life. Like Tim, they turn to God at the last minute, hoping that He is there and will come to their aid, instead of developing a relationship with Him. As in all relationships, to truly develop a deep, intimate relationship with God requires an investment of time and of our hearts. But how do you get started?

You may be thinking, "How can I trust God—I can't even see Him?" or "You have no idea what I have done. I can't go to God. He wants nothing to do with me." Friend, I assure you, nothing could be further from the truth! I may not know what you have gone through or what you have done that is gripping your heart with guilt, but God does. There is no hope in trying to hide it from Him or even trying to hide yourself from Him. He already knows what you have done. He already knows what struggles you have been through. He stands at the edge of your life and gently calls to you, "My child, let Me be a part of your life!" He will not intrude into your life, for He is a true gentleman. He will continue to gently pursue you until you turn to Him for comfort.

If developing a relationship with God were simply based on our actions and a set of rules that we are to keep, nobody would be able to measure up. That is the whole point of the Gospel message! Jesus didn't come into this world to condemn you for not following the rules, or for wandering into the desert of your life, but to provide a way back to God—to build a bridge back to Him. He came so that we may have life, and have it abundantly! (See John 10:10 NKJV.)

So how do we cross the bridge? How do you find your way from the middle of your desert where all you see is dry, hot sand that burns your feet, and a hot sun that wears you down? How do you find your way? Jesus said, "I am the way, the truth and the life" (John 14:6).

God already knows what you have done in your past. But do you know what He has already done for you? We have broken God's law. Just as in our society, if we break a law, there is a penalty; if we break God's law there is also a penalty. The Bible says that the result of sin is death (Rom. 6:23). When we break God's law, we deserve death—eternal separation from God.

God is a holy, just God, and requires that someone pay the penalty for breaking His law. When Jesus walked the earth, He perfectly kept all of God's laws, living a perfect life. Even though He did not deserve death, He accepted your penalty and died in your place (2 Cor. 5:21). He was brutally beaten, was nailed to and died on a cross and went to Hell, then rose from the dead three days later so that you would have the chance to go to Heaven to be with God.

The Bible says that He became sin for us so that we may receive His righteousness (2 Cor. 5:21). He invites you to accept what He has already done for you as payment for your sins. If you have never done this, you can do it right now by simply confessing your sins to God (agreeing with Him that you have sinned), repenting (turning away from sin), and accepting what Jesus has done for you. You are asking that God would credit Jesus' work to you. A suggested prayer is below.

God is interested in your heart. God will honor your prayer. The words are not important. He wants you to come out of the desert and to have a spring of life flowing within you (John 7:38). I encourage you to take a moment and evaluate your life. Have you taken the time to recognize that you have not lived up to God's standards? Have you personally asked Jesus to come into your life and forgive your sins? Friend, it is the most important thing you will ever do! I encourage you, if you have never done so, to go before God and acknowledge that you are a sinner and ask Jesus to come into your life and make you a new person—a new creation—a part of His family! (See 2 Cor. 5:17.)

Lord Jesus, I need You. Thank You for dying on the cross for my sins. I open the door of my life and receive You as my Savior and Lord. Thank You for forgiving my sins and giving me eternal life.

Take control of my life. Make me the kind of person You want me to be. Amen.

Did you pray that prayer? If so, I welcome you into the family of God! Today is truly a special day and one you will never forget! In the next chapter we will look at what it means to be part of the body of Christ and what your new spiritual birth means for you! Please contact a local pastor or *Campus Crusade for Christ* to receive materials on how to grow in your new faith! You can go to *www.jesuswho.org/english/nowthat.htm* to find out your next steps as a Christian and to request life-changing materials. I hope you will take that next step and find out how to live your life abiding in Him—fulfilling your destiny of discipleship.

If you have been a Christian who, like many, has fallen into complacency in your spiritual walk, you can renew your commitment to Him right now by once again submitting your life to His Lordship. Jesus told how a shepherd would leave his flock of 99 sheep to go out and seek after the one that was missing. Right now He is calling to you, desiring that you would come back into His fold. Ask Him to forgive you for the times of complacency and rebellion, and to refresh your walk with Him. He will be faithful to answer your prayer and breathe new life into you.

> Tim was already half an hour late for work when he glanced at his watch. Time had flown by. But it was worth it! He could actually feel that a great weight had been lifted from him. He wanted to know more. Pastor Steve gave him a Bible and some material to read through. "Can I stop by tomorrow?" Tim asked eagerly.
>
> "Sure. I'd love to see you again. Same time is fine with me. Feel free to stop in any day you'd like and chat during lunch," Pastor Steve said. "I would

like to meet with you at least once or twice a week to help you get started with your new journey. You have an incredible future ahead of you. God has some amazing plans for you, Tim. I can feel it."

Pastor Steve watched Tim leave and walk down the street with a new spring in his step. The pastor looked up to Heaven and said out loud, "I'm not sure what You have planned for him, Lord. But I'm glad I can at least be here for the start of it."

Reflection

In what areas are you trying to be independent from God?

1.

2.

3.

If you have just asked Jesus Christ to be your Savior, list three things that you hope will be different now that you have Him in your life.

1.

2.

3.

If you have been walking with Jesus Christ for a while, list three things that you have seen change as a result of your relationship with Him.

1.

2.

3.

CHAPTER 2
BECOMING PART OF THE FAMILY OF GOD

Trying to be independent doesn't work. We are dependent on countless people. But we are also dependent on God! Whether we recognize it or not, God is involved in our lives in a deep, personal way. Many times we don't stop and think about how much God is involved in our lives. We are too busy "living" to stop and see that we are living because of Him, not because of something we have done. The Bible tells us "apart from [Christ] you can do nothing" (John 15:5). You may say, "Wait a minute! I can do lots of things without God." And you could probably list a series of tasks you have accomplished "without" God's help.

God is a sovereign God, allowing what will fulfill His purposes and putting a stop to things that will come in the way of His perfect will. If you could accomplish something that God did not want you to, what kind of a God would He be? If your will had the power to overrule God's, why worship Him? The fact is that everything we do must first pass through God's hands to be allowed.

We have such a distorted view of who God is. We can't grasp the unimaginable power that He has, and the extremely limited amount of power that we have as His creatures. Look around sometime at the massive mountains, sprawling fields, rushing streams, and expansive oceans full of living creatures. All that and more is in front of your eyes because He spoke. He didn't get out His tools and work up a sweat and construct it through hard labor. He simply spoke and it was. We can't fathom the power that our God possesses. Yet, even though we are His creatures, He desires to bring us into His family and allow us to share in His glory. It is simply amazing!

Our culture seems to teach us the reverse! We are taught that whatever we want is what we should have. We are the masters of our own fate. We hold the keys to our own destiny. I assure you, His will for our lives shall come to pass.

So what does that mean practically for us as believers? What is our role in fulfilling His will for our lives? Well, as part of His family, we have been given an amazing gift! Not only did we receive eternal life through God's grace, we have been made His children. We all have one Father and are heirs to His kingdom. We are no longer to be part of this world, but ambassadors to it.

Our role is to get in line with God's will in our own lives, and follow His guidance. Jesus said, "Whoever loses his life for my sake will find it" (Matt 10:39). Our lives, as believers, are not our own. We have been bought with a price—the blood of Jesus Christ. We are not independent at all. We are completely dependent on God and interdependent on other believers as we experience this short-lived life.

The church—the body of Christ—is the perfect example of interdependence. The Bible tells us that we have been given different gifts, but are part of the same body. And even though we are all part of one body, we each have a different function to perform (Rom 12:4-8). When you become a part of God's family, you have a role to fulfill—a destiny. You have been given gifts and talents that *need* to be used so that others may be blessed. We all have a responsibility to use our gifts so that the rest of the body is strengthened. When we use our gifts within the body, it functions better and more efficiently.

Thursday morning as Tim walked past that little white church, he was thinking about what had happened. Last night when he got home, he had read the materials Pastor Steve had given him, and was fascinated! Why hadn't someone told him all of this years ago? He began to read the Gospel of John, just as Pastor Steve had suggested. It was actually making sense to him. He smiled as he saw his new friend in the side yard of the church, and called to him with a new excitement in his voice. "Good morning, Pastor Steve! I'll see you today at lunch."

Pastor Steve smiled and returned the wave. "I'm looking forward to it!"

Time seemed to stand still that morning. Tim watched the clock, waiting for noon so he could go ask Pastor Steve his questions. As noon approached, Stan, his boss, came into his office and sat down.

"We have a new client coming in today. I need you to come to lunch with us to meet him. He wants to meet us at noon down the road at Mama Mia's, that little Italian place. This could be a big client for us." As he got up and walked out of his office, Tim was excited and disappointed at the same time. His hard work for the firm was paying off. The long days of being little more than a gofer were finally paying the dividends they had promised. He hoped that Pastor Steve would understand. Maybe they could meet tomorrow. This was his job, how could he say no?

As the minutes and hours slipped by, Pastor Steve began to wonder where Tim was. As he waited, he began to prepare his lesson for Sunday. He thought that he should speak on God's Grace this week. They had just finished a six-week study on stewardship and godly money management. People seemed to really enjoy the lesson, but this week he wanted to get back to the basics. As he was putting the finishing touches on his sermon, he heard a knock at the door. As he walked toward the side door, he could see Tim standing outside with a disappointed look on his face.

"What's wrong, Tim?"

"I'm sorry about today, Pastor Steve. I was in my office and..." As Tim tried to explain his reason for not coming to lunch, Pastor Steve remembered a passage that he was just looking at for his sermon.

"Son," he interrupted, "you need to remember that 'There is no condemnation for those who are in Christ Jesus.' You don't have to give me an explanation. It's all right. I'm just glad that you are here now. Come on in." Tim was a little shocked. *Doesn't he care where I was? Or how my day was? Or why I didn't show up,* he thought. As he sat down in Pastor Steve's office, still a little dazed by his comment, Pastor Steve pressed, "Now, tell me how your day was." *Okay, so he does care. But what did he mean by that condemnation thing?*

"Well," Tim started, "I got invited to go to lunch with a new client."

"Congratulations!" Pastor Steve exclaimed.

"Well, it gets better," Tim went on to explain. "As we were sitting at the restaurant waiting for the client to arrive, I got talking with my boss. He told me that the business manager is leaving in about six months; and that if I can prove myself by then, he will give me that job and hire an assistant for me! I was thinking, maybe it's God helping me out or something. What do you think?"

"I think you might be right, Tim. God is a gracious, giving God. He loves you and wants to give you good gifts. So how did the lunch go?"

"It was pretty boring. This new client was more interested in himself than anything else. We all had to act like he was a great guy so he would give us his case. It was pretty sickening."

Pastor Steve replied, "I'm sure it was. Did you get a chance to look at the material I gave you last night?"

Tim brightened. "Yes! It was pretty amazing stuff. I started reading Luke, too. I never got it before, but it really made sense last night." He paused. "I have to ask you something. What did you mean by that condemnation comment when I came in?"

Pastor Steve explained, "Well, the Bible tells us that there is no condemnation for those who are in Christ. That means that those of us who accept the gift of salvation through what He did at the cross will have no penalty to pay for their own sins because the penalty was paid by Jesus."

"Oh! I wasn't exactly paying attention when I walked in. All I heard was something about condemnation, and I was a little confused about what you were talking about. That makes sense," Tim said, relieved.

"You know, Tim, so many people around the world believe that all roads will lead them to Heaven. For years I have fought this idea using scripture that speaks about Jesus being the only way to God. But recently I had a revelation. Now I completely agree with their statement."

"What?" Tim asked, with a confused look on his face. This was completely opposite of everything he had just read last night.

"Well," Pastor Steve continued, "what happens when our physical bodies die? Where does our soul go?"

"To Heaven?" Tim asked, wondering where he was going with this.

"Right! For us who have accepted Jesus as our Lord and Savior," Pastor Steve replied, looking at Tim, as if he was waiting for him to say something. "What about those who didn't accept Christ?" Pastor Steve continued.

"Well, I guess they go to Hell," Tim responded.

"Right again." Again he paused.

Tim finally asked, "Well, how is that ending up at the same place?"

Pastor Steve smiled. "I'm glad you asked! We all die. Agreed? And when we die, one of two things happens. Those who have accepted Jesus as Lord and Savior will stand before the judgment seat of Jesus Christ and be judged on their deeds, both good and bad (2 Cor. 5:10). Those who have not accepted His gift of salvation will stand before the throne of God and be judged according to their deeds and then cast into eternal punishment (Rev. 20:12-15). So, at one point we all, regardless of our religious beliefs, will stand before the Lord and be judged. Where we go after that—that's the question! And the answer is found in our response to the Gospel."

Tim sat in deep thought a minute, then, trying to break the heaviness that lingered in the room, he asked, "So, how was your day?"

"I had a nice day. I got a lot of work done," Pastor Steve answered. "By the way, I wanted to invite you to come join us on Sunday for our worship service. It starts at 11:00 and goes until about 12:30. I think you'll enjoy it. There are a lot of people your age there. You really need to get involved in a church as soon as you can, Tim. It is vital to living the Christian life. Even though salvation is a free gift, living out our salvation takes work."

"Sure," Tim replied happily. "I'll come Sunday. You're not going to have me introduce myself or anything, right?"

Pastor Steve laughed. "Not at all. And you don't even have to come here to this church. I would love it if you did, but as long as you are involved in a good, Bible teaching church, that's what matters most. It's the fellowship with other believers that's important. We all need each other in the Body." He went on to explain, "We're like a football team. Not everyone on the team does the same thing, but they are all important to the game. In the church, not all of us have the same gift or the same role, but together we make up one body, Christ's body, here on earth. We all need each other. That's the way God made us."

How are we to live so that we are dependent on God and interdependent on other believers? The first step is to get involved in a local church that is preaching the finished work of Jesus Christ. We need the help of our brothers and sisters in order to make our walk with Christ a fruitful journey. Too many times Christianity is a weekend habit, not a lifestyle. Get involved with a small group at your church. If they do not have a small group program, start one. We need others in our lives who will encourage and motivate us.

The journey that we are on is not an easy one. Without a support structure of other believers, it is like trying to hike to the top of a new mountain without a guide. Our Christian journey is walked on a narrow road (Matt. 7:14). Be sure to take a guide with you—someone who can help you as you navigate through the pitfalls of life. We all need someone who will celebrate with us at the peaks in life and someone who will console us in the valleys. We need our brothers and sisters to keep us accountable.

Have you ever flown somewhere and looked out the window? The placid blue sky and fluffy clouds make a beautiful picture. But what would happen if the pilots didn't notice that their compass and other instruments weren't working properly? Even if their instruments were off by one degree, you wouldn't end up where you wanted to be. It is the same in our walk with Christ. Without someone there to keep us accountable, we can take small turns that we think don't matter, but in the long run we will find ourselves in a place where we definitely don't want to be. Taking one step off the path leads to taking another and another. Soon we will be living in such a way that our life and our Christian beliefs are like night and day. But having someone you trust and respect act as a "check" for your walk is a huge blessing. They can objectively see you taking steps off the path that you may not see. Get someone in your life who can be your accountability partner.

What else does being part of God's family mean? Along with being there for one another during life's hard times and joyous times, we are given an amazing promise. Jesus said "For where two or three come together in my name, there am I with them" (Matt. 18:20). We are His children, and He desires to be with us and to spend time with us. He has promised that when we gather in His name, He will honor that gathering with His presence. We are called to be in community with other believers. We are called to celebrate and worship together, to make our requests known to Him and to expect that He will answer our prayers according to His perfect will.

I have talked to so many people who are convinced that they do not need to go to church. They have a "personal" faith. As Christians, we all have a personal faith. We have the Spirit of the Creator dwelling within us. Even though we don't "need" to go to church to be saved, for that is through faith in Christ alone, we do need the fellowship of our brothers and sisters in our lives.

The early believers "...devoted...themselves to...fellowship..." (Acts 2:42). They were facing persecution that we can't imagine. In some countries, like China, persecution is still continuing as it was in the days of Christ. People are tortured and murdered for their faith in Christ almost daily. Why is it that during times when believers are being persecuted for their faith and for gathering together, they continue to have worship and fellowship with one another; but when we have the freedom to meet and worship without fear of persecution, we simply don't? Maybe it's because we don't understand the precious gift we have been given. We don't understand that by being with one another, we experience the power of God Himself.

We are able to be His hands and feet to others. The gifts we have received are to be used to build up the members of the body and to increase it in numbers. God's will is for everyone to come to the saving knowledge of Christ (Rom. 10:1). By sharing our experiences with one another, strengthening one another and helping each other go out and reach the world, we are accomplishing His purposes. Jesus said, "Whoever does God's will is my brother and sister..." (Mark 3:35). But doing the will of the Father is not accomplished alone. We need the body as much as the body needs us. It is this interdependency that makes the body such a gift.

We are all called to go into the world and make disciples. The great commission found in Matthew 28:18-20 tells us we are to "...go and make disciples of all nations…teaching them to obey everything I have commanded you. And surely I am with you always, to the very end of the age." We cannot do this work alone. And we have not been called to go to church on Sunday, sit in a seat and watch as others "in ministry" do all the work. Christianity is NOT a spectator sport. Unfortunately, in today's culture, as someone once put it, "Christianity is like football. You have 22 men on the field who desperately need a break and 22,000 in the stands who desperately need exercise." That was not the intent when Jesus gave this command. He wants the whole church to participate in building the body and in worshipping. We can't afford to sit back and put our minds and hearts on autopilot. Get off the bleachers of life and get into the greatest "game" ever played—your new life—a life abiding in Christ!

Reflection

Think back to your childhood. What are some of your favorite memories of your father?

What are some favorite memories of your mother?

How has God used your natural family to shadow your spiritual family?

How can you be more involved in God's family through your local church?

1.

2.

3.

Who is someone you can trust to hold you accountable to continue in your walk with Jesus Christ?

Call that person and set up a regular time to get together and discuss your walk with the Lord.

CHAPTER 3
WORSHIP

It was a rainy Monday morning as Tim passed by the church once again. He had gone there Sunday for worship and was amazed at what he found. He found a group of people who loved God and each other, and was able to express that love through songs and fellowship like he had not seen before.

A band, he thought when he arrived. *What are they doing with a band? Maybe something special is going on today.* He remembered the cold, almost sterile environment that he was used to seeing in a church. A large pipe organ or a piano—yes, but a whole band in church?

As he waited for the service to begin, he was greeted by what seemed to be hundreds of new people. They all introduced themselves and welcomed him to the church. *Pastor Steve must have asked them to say hi to me*, he thought. *People aren't usually this friendly in church.*

At the beginning of the service, he felt uncomfortable and a little nervous. He was in a new place, meeting so many new people, and not sure what to expect. But he found himself enthralled in the praise and worship time. The songs seemed to speak exactly what was on his heart. Tears welled up in his eyes as he sang words written by someone else but from his own heart at the same time.

As Pastor Steve spoke, his message was interesting, funny, and actually made sense. Tim watched the people around him as Steve spoke. They were paying attention to Steve, not looking at their watches. Tim felt a peace that he hadn't felt before. He was home. Somehow he knew that this was where he needed to be, not just today, but for a long time. Time seemed to fly by.

Afterward everyone gathered for coffee and pastries in the fellowship hall. Here Tim received many more introductions and "welcomes!" He was a little overwhelmed and hoped that nobody would expect him to remember their name next week. As he walked to his car, he felt a peace and refreshment that he hadn't found in a long time. He was definitely home.

What do you think of when you hear the word "worship"? For many in churches around the world, the image of corporate singing of hymns and songs of praise, and lifting our hands to the Lord come to mind. While this can be an outward demonstration of our feelings of love, admiration and awe toward our God, we are called to a deeper, more fulfilling act that involves not only our voices, but also our whole being.

The Merriam-Webster dictionary defines worship as: *reverence offered a divine being.* In the New International Version, the term worship (or forms of the word, such as worshipped and worshipping) is used 251 times. It is used 75 times in the New Testament alone. With this word being used so often in Scripture and our modern church services focusing largely on worship, why is it that we haven't studied the meaning of the actual words used in the original Biblical writings?

Many people don't realize that when the original writings were being translated, there were many words (at least 11 from the Greek alone) that were translated into our English word "worship." Below is a list of some of those Greek and Hebrew words. This list is adapted from *Praise and Worship, a Greek and Hebrew word study,* by Dr. Paul Vickers, Eat the Word, 1992-2001 available at http://www.eattheword.com/downloadables/WordStudy.pdf

Read through the definitions and passages which show the context of each word. I believe you will begin to get a much broader sense of what true worship is.

Ethelothracekiah - Voluntary (arbitrary and unwarranted) piety, i.e. sanctimony

Such regulations indeed have an appearance of wisdom, with their self-imposed **worship**, *their false humility and their harsh treatment of the body, but they lack any value in restraining sensual indulgence.* Col. 2:23

Eusebeo - To be pious towards God; or (towards parents) respect

For as I walked around and looked carefully at your objects of **worship**, *I even found an altar with this inscription: TO AN UNKNOWN GOD. Now what you* **worship** *as something unknown I am going to proclaim to you.* Acts 17:23

Theosebace - Reverent of God, i.e. pious

Now we know that God does not hear sinners: but if any one is a **worshipper** *of God, and does His will, He hears him.* John 9:31 (NKJV)

Therapeuo - To wait upon menially, i.e. to adore God; to cure, heal, worship

"Nor is He **worshipped** *[served] with men's hands, as though He needed anything, since He gives to all life, and breath, and all things."* Acts 17:25 (NKJV)

When Jesus had called the Twelve together, he gave them power and authority to drive out all demons and to **cure** *diseases.* Luke 9:1

Thraceki'ah - Ceremonial observance

Do not let anyone who delights in false humility and the **worship** *of angels disqualify you for the prize. Such a person goes into great detail about what he has seen, and his unspiritual mind puffs him up with idle notions.* Col. 2:18

Religion *that God our Father accepts as pure and faultless is this: to look after orphans and widows in their distress and to keep oneself from being polluted by the world.* James 1:27

Lat-ryoo-o - To minister to God, i.e. render religious homage

"But God turned away and gave them over to the **worship** *of the heavenly bodies."* Acts 7:42

I thank God, whom I **serve**, *as my forefathers did, with a clear conscience, as night and day I constantly remember you in my prayers.* 2 Tim. 1:3

Neokoros - A temple servant; worshipper

And when the townclerk had appeased the people, he said, "Ye men of Ephesus, what man is there that knoweth not how that the city of the Ephesians is a **worshipper** *of the great goddess Diana, and of the image which fell down from Jupiter?"* Acts 19:35 (KJV)

Proskuneo - to kiss the hand to (towards) one, in token of reverence, like a dog licking his master's hand; to fawn or crouch; to prostrate oneself in homage, do reverence to, adore. It is the most widely used word translated into worship. According to *The Strongest Strong's Exhaustive Concordance of the Bible*, James Strong, Zondervan, 2001, it was used 60 times in the New Testament.

And asked, "Where is the one who has been born king of the Jews? We saw his star in the east and have come to **worship** *him."* Matt. 2:2

Jesus said to him, "Away from me, Satan! For it is written: **'Worship** *the Lord your God, and serve him only.'"* Matt. 4:10

"God is spirit, and his **worshippers** *must* **worship** *in spirit and in truth."* John 4:24

Seb-ad'zom-ahee - To revere

They exchanged the truth of God for a lie, and **worshipped** *and served created things rather than the Creator—who is forever praised. Amen.* Rom. 1:25

Sebasma - Something adored, i.e. an object of worship.

He will oppose and will exalt himself over everything that is called God or is **worshipped**, *so that he sets himself up in God's temple, proclaiming himself to be God.* 2 Thess. 2:4

Seb'-om-ahee - To revere, i.e. adore

"'They **worship** *me in vain; their teachings are but rules taught by men.'"* Matt. 15:9

Segiyd - Worship, to prostrate oneself (in homage)

"As soon as you hear the sound of the horn, flute, zither, lyre, harp, pipes and all kinds of music, you must fall down and **worship** *the image of gold that King Nebuchadnezzar has set up."* Dan. 3:5

Atsav - To carve, i.e. fabricate or fashion; (in a bad sense) to worry, pain or anger

The women also said, "And when we burned incense to the queen of heaven, and poured out drink offerings to her, did we make cakes for her, to **worship** *her, and pour out drink offerings to her, without our husbands' permission?"* Jer. 44:19 (NKJV)

"And his father had not **displeased** *him at any time...."* 1 Kings 1:6 (KJV)

"...that Thou wouldst keep me from harm, that it may not **grieve** *me...."* 1 Chron. 4:10 (KJV)

"...Do not **grieve**, *for the joy of the LORD is your strength."* Neh. 8:10

Shachah - To depress, i.e. to prostrate in homage to royalty or God

He said to his servants, "Stay here with the donkey while I and the boy go over there. We will **worship** *and then we will come back to you."* Gen. 22:5

"Do not **worship** *any other god, for the LORD, whose name is Jealous, is a jealous God."* Ex. 34:14

"May nations serve you and peoples **bow down** *to you."* Gen. 27:29

All kings will **bow down** *to him and all nations will serve him.* Ps. 72:11

All the royal officials at the king's gate knelt down and **paid honor** *to Haman....* Esther 3:2

As you can see, the meaning of the original Biblical words for "worship" mean far more than raising our voices in song to God. As a matter of fact, none of the above definitions mention music or singing. This is not to say that using songs is not appropriate in the worshipping of God. It is recorded that Moses used songs during worship in the Old Testament. It is just an observation that our contemporary understanding of what worship is, and how God intends us to understand it through the Scripture, is different.

What does Jesus have to say about worship? In John 4:23-24, Jesus says to the Samaritan woman at the well, "Yet a time is coming and has now come when the true worshippers will worship the Father in spirit and truth, for they are the kind of worshippers the Father seeks. God is spirit, and his worshippers must worship in spirit and in truth." What does He mean by "in Spirit and in Truth"? This concept is so important that He repeats it to her. Wouldn't it make sense for us to learn what Jesus meant by "in spirit and in truth" since "they are the kind of worshippers the Father seeks"?

First, let's look at what He meant by "in Spirit." The original Greek term used here by Jesus for "worship" is "proskuneo," meaning "to kiss the hand towards one, in token of reverence, to fawn or crouch; to prostrate oneself in homage; do reverence to; adore." It seems that God desires us to show our love, admiration and respect for Him through signs of adoration, not only through singing. In short, He desires us to put Him in His proper place—not only as Lord of Lords and King of Kings, but the true Lord of *our lives*—not just Sunday mornings—but every day. We are to live out every part of our lives with Him on the throne, and us as His servants, giving Him the proper respect and authority that He deserves.

In Romans chapter 12, we are encouraged that truly living the Christian life and keeping our bodies and our lives pure is an act of *spiritual* worship. Paul admonishes us to stay steadfast in our understanding of the Gospel and not to allow the world to corrupt us. This comes right after he has just talked about how the Jews have “stumbled” in their relationship and understanding of God’s provision of salvation. We are to learn from them and live so that we will not become “hardened” to God. Jesus knew we could not do that on our own. We need the Holy Spirit to be our guide throughout our Christian life.

We need to rely on the Holy Spirit to keep our hearts focused on His will. In Romans 8:26 we are told that the Spirit will join with our spirit in making requests and petitions to God. In essence, when we don’t even know how or what to pray, the Spirit intercedes for us and makes our requests known to God the Father, in accordance with the will of God. We are told in James 4:3 that we make requests of God and do not receive because our intentions are not in line with God’s will. If we rely on the aid and direction of the Spirit on a daily basis, we will not have that happen. We will search out the things of God and ask for those things in our lives. There may even be times when we don’t humanly understand why we are asking for them or why we are praying for something. At these times, it is the Spirit guiding us. We need to embrace these times and allow the Spirit to be in command. For what better act of worship is there than giving God full control and access to our lives?

What about worshipping *in truth*? John 14:6 tells us that *Jesus* is “the way, the *truth* and the life.” So Jesus needs to be the central focus of our worship. This may sound overly simplified, but are we too often going through the motions in our church services, not putting our heart and soul into our worship? At these times, what are we worshipping? If we are not fully engaged spiritually and mentally in our worship, can we be truthfully worshipping? At times when we are not fully engaged in spiritual worship, we become as the Pharisees had become—a group so interested in keeping every letter of the law, that they completely missed the fact that God loved them and wanted to be in relationship with them. Over the years, they made their act of adoration and thanksgiving to God a series of ceremonies that had lost meaning. In Matthew 15:9 it says, "They worship me in vain; their teachings are but rules taught by men." Sometimes this is what happens in churches today. We do a great job going through actions of worship and "putting in time," but are we really worshipping with our heart?

How many of us are doing the same thing in our own lives? How many times have we left our church and felt as though God didn't "show up" today? We didn't feel His presence, we weren't touched by the sermon, we weren't aware of the needs in our lives that He desired to fill through others around us. We went through the motions, but didn't experience His loving presence. Maybe we were thinking about what we needed to do for work that week, or about family concerns, etc. It isn't that God didn't show up. It is that WE didn't show up spiritually and emotionally. If we don't spiritually show up, we aren't able to worship Him in truth.

Worshipping in *truth* is tied to understanding that Jesus is Lord of all, especially of our lives. If we really understood the truth about Jesus—who He really is, we would drop everything in our lives and run after Him with all our might. The truth of worship is that He is everything we need and nothing that we don't.

Through Him we can accomplish our destiny in life. Without Him we cannot fulfill it.

In Exodus 33:18-22, Moses asked God to reveal His glory to him. In order to do so, God put Moses in a cave, covered the opening with His hand and then walked by. Why didn't God simply reveal Himself to Moses and show Himself in His glory? We are told that if Moses saw God's face, he would die! Moses was only allowed to see the back of God after He walked past. Jesus is one with God and is just as glorious and wonderful as the Father. When we worship Jesus in truth, we realize that He is the supreme ruler, the creator, and we are the creatures. We need to remember that even though we have been counted as heirs to the throne of grace, we are still His servant-children. We have no right, in any way, to think that we *deserve* to be in the throne room with God, for it is by grace, which is UN-merited favor, that we are able to be called His children.

What is our response to Him when we consider these things? I am curious what we would do if, when in the middle of a worship service, we were confronted with the full glory of who Jesus is in bodily form. I truly doubt that we would all stand and in unison simply sing a pre-recorded song. I think we would be on our faces praising Him for what He has done for us and showing Him that He is far above us in His worth and honor. Why is it that many of us do not have that same reaction when we experience Him in spiritual form? We are so used to the idea that the Spirit of God lives in us that sometimes we get immune or complacent to the awe of what that truly means. We take for granted the incomprehensible power and majesty that is God—in us.

In what other ways can we worship? Many churches invite members to give their tithes and offerings as an act of worship. Is this in line with the Biblical model? I believe it can be, but is it for most of us? When we give our tithe, what are we saying? Are we trying to give our "payment" to the church for the service that week, or are we communicating that our relationship with God is more important than what we could use this money for? Although we have no direct command in the New Testament to give a tithe to the church, we see in 2 Corinthians 8 that Paul urges us to be "generous" in giving. Also, in chapter 9 he makes it clear that we will receive from God in direct proportion to what we give to His work.

This seems like the word "generous" could be ambiguous and depend on the individual's opinion of what "generous" is. As you look at the time and place that Paul is in when he writes these words, we see that the "norm" in his day was to give over 20% of your income to the work of God. The custom was to give a tithe of 10%, a temple tax, and to leave a percentage of your crops un-harvested for the poor. With this being the standard or norm, he writes that we are to be generous. If this is what Paul is referring to as generous, will a lower amount suffice?

Many believers argue that we are no longer "under the Law." While this is true as far as following the Law to gain salvation, they use this approach to validate the idea of not giving a tithe. When Jesus gave us the Sermon on the Mount, He raised the bar on the Law. He said many times, "you have heard this…but I say to you this…," each time calling us to an even more radical understanding of what He intends for and from our lives.

As to tithing, He is not necessarily looking for us to have a certain percentage that we give to His work. He is looking for us to realize that what we have is 100% His and we are merely stewards of it. We are to give generously "on every occasion" (2 Cor. 9:11). It seems that we are called to give even MORE than a tithe. It is not a matter of giving a certain amount and being "done" with our giving. We are called to give on a constant basis to those in need and to fulfill our role in His work. When we let go of a percentage to give and become willing to give Him everything, I believe we start to worship God with our offering.

How else can we worship in *Spirit* and in *truth*? In Romans 12:1-2, we are told, "...I urge you, brothers, in view of God's mercy, to offer your bodies as living sacrifices, holy and pleasing to God—this is your spiritual act of worship. Do not conform any longer to the pattern of this world, but be transformed by the renewing of your mind." How can we do this? What are the requirements for this type of worship? Paul goes on to list several things that we are not to do, encouraging us to be different from the world around us. We are to be renewed by the truth of the Gospel and to live out that truth in our lives. We are to love and meet the needs of others, give generously, and live in harmony with others. In short, we need to become a reflection of who God is. We need to become the "light" in the "darkness" that Jesus talked about.

When we live this way, we are putting the will of God above our own. We need to use our lives—our actions, words and attitudes—as a sacrificial gift to God. Not only as a sacrifice, but as a *holy* sacrifice. We need to do these things not based on our own ego or pride, but truly based on the relationship we have with God through Jesus. Our motivation for these actions can come from ourselves at times. The good feeling we get from giving or helping someone in need can motivate us to repeat our "good deed." This is not acceptable as worship. Our worship through our lives is not based on actions and deeds, but on the underlying motivation for those actions. When our deeds are a result of our striving to live out our relationships with Jesus, we begin to worship God through our lives.

All this is not to say that singing is not important and should not be a part of our worship. We are told in Colossians 3:16 that we are to "Let the word of Christ dwell in you richly as you teach and admonish one another with all wisdom, and as you sing psalms, hymns and spiritual songs with gratitude in your hearts to God." Likewise in Ephesians 5:18-20, we see that we are to "...be filled with the Spirit. Speak to one another with psalms, hymns and spiritual songs. Sing and make music in your heart to the Lord, always giving thanks to God the Father for everything, in the name of our Lord Jesus Christ."

We see from these passages that singing songs of praise and thanksgiving are important, even encouraged by Paul. In both Colossians and Ephesians we are told to sing songs that honor God and show our thankfulness for the grace and mercy He has bestowed on us. The Psalms are a wonderful collection of songs of praise to God. But why do we sing? When we sing, are we considering the awe of *who* we are singing to, or are we more concerned about our voices and staying in tune? Let us take time and reflect on how God desires us to worship and strive to fulfill His design.

As a member of His body, take a look at our practice of worship and be sure that we are in line with the teaching of Jesus. We need to be worshippers of Him in Spirit and in Truth. God does not accept going though the motions as worship. Merely singing some songs on Sunday is not acceptable. He demands more from us. He demands us to be totally engaged in the act of daily worship in our lives. We are to do everything we do as an act of worship to our God. Every action, every word, every decision should be an act of letting God know that we recognize Him as the ruler of our life and that He alone is worthy of worship. Letting the Spirit have the reins of our life and allowing Him to direct our steps and guide our paths, I believe, is spiritual and truthful worship—worship from your heart. For Jesus warns us in Mark 7:6-7 that we should be careful not to be like the hypocrites who "honor me with their lips, but their hearts are far from me. They worship me in vain; their teachings are but rules taught by men."

Reflection

What are three ways that you express your worship to God?

1.
2.
3.

How can you make worship a daily activity in your life?

CHAPTER 4
UNDERSTANDING GOD'S HEART

It was a chilly morning in October. The brightly colored leaves slowly fell to the ground as a gentle breeze blew. As Tim walked past the familiar church once more, he saw Pastor Steve in the side yard raking leaves into a huge pile. He remembered how his dad used to let him jump into the massive piles when he was a boy. Pastor Steve had become for him a sort of stepfather over the past few months. He valued their friendship and his wisdom. Unfortunately, since business had picked up for Tim, their friendly get-togethers had been reduced to a once-every-other-week lunch meeting. He had learned so much from meeting with Pastor Steve and from his personal studies. He missed getting together more often and was grieved that he didn't have as much time now to study on his own.

Pastor Steve had assured Tim that God's economy isn't like the world's economy, that even if he couldn't meet as often and didn't have time to do as much studying as he used to, he would still be an adored child of God. "It's not what we do for God that is credited to us as righteousness, but what He has done for us that counts," Pastor Steve had said. "That's not to say that we shouldn't study and be in close relationship with Jesus; but when our study time and devotional life become taskmasters, we have lost the point. Following Christ isn't about a list of rules and 'putting in time' as much as it is finding the heartbeat of God and following that." He shared how the Pharisees were more concerned with following rules than finding God's heart behind the rules.

"That makes sense, but how do you know where the balance is? How do you know what God's heartbeat is?" Tim had asked.

Pastor Steve answered, "Well, Tim, we need to make sure our focus is on knowing God and His will for us, not just knowing His rules. We can follow all the rules and still miss having a relationship with God Himself. And without that, everything else is useless. His heart is to know you and for you to know Him, not just His rules. He desires to be your friend, your closest companion. The more you study His word, the more you will find out about His heart; and then you'll want to follow His rules, not out of duty but out of respect and love."

So many people know about Jesus but never know Him. You may have been or maybe are one right now who knows a lot about Jesus but has never taken time to start an intimate, personal relationship with Him. I encourage you to do so now. You may say "What's the difference?" Well, let me explain.

As Pastor Steve had earlier explained to Tim, you may know who the president is and even know a lot about him. You may know about his childhood, his likes and dislikes. You may know where he is from, where he went to high school and college, and when he started his political career. You may know his dog's name, his favorite color, his favorite food and so on. Does this knowledge that you have about him make you a close friend to him? Do he and his wife come to your house for dinner because you know enough details about them? Does he call you to play a round of golf or watch a sporting event once you get to know enough details about his life? Of course not! Knowing *about* a person is different than knowing that person—being their friend.

It is the same with God. He is a person! You need to get to know Him, not just details about him. In chapter one, I outlined the way to start an intimate relationship with God through accepting Jesus, His son, as the sacrifice for your sin. He is the only way to obtain salvation (John 14:6; Acts 4:12). Simply knowing about God—His rules and stories about what He has done—does not save you. Going to church on Sunday does not save you. Doing good works does not save you.

The only way is through a relationship with Christ by faith. He is not interested in what you do for Him, for He can do it all Himself. He is not interested in having you sit in a church for a couple hours each week and having the rest of your life not reflect Christ to the world. He is interested in changing your heart and conforming you to His image through your intimate walk with Him. He doesn't just want your time, your money, or your lip service. He wants your heart. He wants 100% of you.

Jesus was often questioned by the Pharisees concerning the laws that governed people's lives. Their focus was on outward experiences or actions. Why is it that in 2000 years we still haven't learned the importance of the heart? Why do we still get caught up in ceremony and our own actions and miss the way that He works in our lives? Maybe it's because in our culture we are so focused on the managing and controlling aspects of life. Our outward activities and customs are things that we can rate, keep track of, and check off our list. We try to walk the Christian walk in an effort to have enough "entries" in our daily journal of "what I have done for God lately." We think that if we accumulate enough of these entries, He will look upon us in a more approving way. Should racking up "points" be the motivation in our lives? The reality is we may look at ourselves that way, but He won't.

This is not a new dilemma! Even the disciples, right after Jesus talked to them about His upcoming persecution and death, argued about who among them was the "greatest." Their concern was in how *they* looked, not about what Jesus was going to do for them. How do we practically live out our lives without feeling that we need to "measure up"? We need to start by looking at what God revealed about us through His Word. Only then will we get a clear understanding of God's heart concerning our role in our sanctification.

If we would start to see ourselves from God's perspective, we would learn so much! Although none of our actions, whether good or bad, are hidden from His eyes, as a believer He looks upon you and sees you covered with the blood and righteousness of Christ. God the Father requires a penalty to be served for sin. Jesus served the guilty sentence that you earned through your sin. There is no way for you to ever earn the righteousness of Christ. It is a free gift that He gives to those who place their trust in Jesus. It is the most amazing gift ever given! All of your sins have been washed away.

Although our actions can never gain our salvation, we are called to live a life with a different set of values than the world around us (Rom. 12:2). We are called to be salt and light (Matt. 5:13-14) to a world that is far from God. We are to be His ambassadors while we are here, to make an eternal difference in people's lives. In doing these things, we need to be sure our motives are right. We need to make sure that we are not trying to "earn points" with God, but are acting out of an overflow from our heart.

When we shine His light into a dark world, we are often criticized and condemned. We are often looked at by the world as bigoted or closed-minded. When you share what Christ has done for you, you are saying a lot about what you value.

Likewise, when we pass up an opportunity to tell someone about who has changed our lives, we are not only being selfish, we are being disobedient. So many times we desire to be accepted and admired by people so much that we are not willing to sacrifice our reputation. Many times it is hard to talk to people about Christ. But that doesn't mean we aren't called to do it. It was hard for Paul to be imprisoned for years. It was hard for the early church when they were being persecuted and killed for their faith. It is still hard today for the persecuted church in areas of the world, such as China, that are still being tortured and put to death for faith in Christ!

Our "hardships" for following Christ in the United States pale in comparison to others around the world. But that doesn't mean that our fears and anxieties are not real. The fear of rejection is a real force that Satan uses to stop us in our tracks. He wants to put the brakes on Christianity so that his kingdom of darkness has the ability to grow.

In Isaiah 9:2 we are told, "The people walking in darkness have seen a great light." This reference is to the coming of Christ. But still today, countless people live in the darkness of having no relationship with God. We are the light. The Spirit of God within us is to shine forth, leading others to God. But what happens when the light is not shining? Jesus said, "No one lights a lamp and hides it in a jar or puts it under a bed. Instead he puts it on a stand, so those who come in can see the light" (Luke 8:16).

We need to walk in a way that our light breaks through the darkness and shines to those around us. We need to overcome the fears we have and be courageous soldiers for Christ. We need to somehow reconcile in our lives that walking with Christ, while it is the most fulfilling thing we can do, is not always the easiest or most fun thing. Many Christians have been hiding their light, not putting their faith on a lampstand, but hiding it from others from fear of persecution. We need to revive our faith in Christ and be stronger now than ever before. We need to make a unified front against the powers of this world and proclaim the Gospel message like never before.

The reason that so many Christians in our country today are worried about sharing their faith is that they fear two main things. The first is a fear that they lack knowledge. They believe that they do not know how to share their faith or know enough about their faith to share it effectively. Secondly, they fear that people, especially friends, family and co-workers will reject them and they will be humiliated. How do I know these are the two major causes? Because not only are they the two that I struggle with myself, but countless individuals in Bible studies and church groups around the country mention them. They seem to be the universal key fears that Satan uses to keep us from spreading the Gospel. These are two of his fiercest weapons! When we learn how to counterattack these weapons, our personal battles with him will be victorious!

The attack of Satan is a real, tangible thing. Our world has watered down the reality of Satan to the point where most people don't believe he even exists. A recent survey conducted by the Barna Group found that six out of ten adults questioned believe that Satan is merely a symbol of evil, not a living being. I am amazed at the number of people who believe in angels and spirits but not demons. We have a distorted image of a demon being an ugly, horned creature that hisses at us and is disgusting to look at. We are told in Ezekiel that the reason for the fall of Lucifer, who by the way was created by God as a beautiful angel, was his desire to be equal with God. He was the most beautiful creature God had made. He and the angels that followed him, one third of the angels to be exact, were cast out of heaven for their sin and betrayal. They are not monstrous, disgusting beasts, but beautiful angels created to worship God and to sing His praises. They are real, living beings with minds, wills and agendas. They know the Scripture and are able to distort it.

Part of the problem with our world today is that we pick and choose what we believe, instead of looking to God and His word for the truth. Later, in chapter eleven, we'll take a closer look at this travesty that has led so many away from God into the hands of Satan himself. Right now, let's look at some truths from Scripture that will show you that Jesus not only believed in the Devil, but He spoke with him and was recognized by demons throughout His ministry.

In Luke 8:28, as Jesus approached a possessed man, the demons recognized Him as "Son of the Most High God" and asked for mercy. How did these demons know who Jesus was? Because He originally created them as angels and they were in heaven with Him. In Luke 4:1-13, we read of the temptation of Jesus by the Devil. It is interesting to notice that Satan knows Scripture extremely well and is able to twist it. He tries to use it to get what he wants from people. We need to be aware that he will sometimes use what appears as godly to pull us away from God Himself. In Matthew 13:36-43, Jesus explains the parable of the weeds, saying that the enemy who sows the bad seeds is the devil. In Mark 9:14-29 we are told of a demon-possessed boy who the disciples could not heal, but Jesus was able to cast out the demon.

These are just a few cases where Scripture talks of casting out demons. We need to remember that demons and Satan are real. They are as real as the air you are breathing. They want you to turn from God. They will stop at nothing. They know exactly what "buttons" to push in your life. One of those "buttons" is fear. It is one of their most effective weapons. Satan uses it to stop you from helping to advance the Kingdom of God so he is freed to advance his kingdom of darkness. We need to be aware of this so we can take action against his forces. We need to stand up as a church and fight back. We need to combat the fears in our lives so that we can stand up to their forces and go forward with the Gospel message. It is not a suggestion, but a direct command to all followers of Christ to "Go out and make disciples of all nations."

Our fears will leave when we understand the heart of God. We need to understand that salvation is something that God desires all humans to enjoy. This is the heart of God. It is our privilege to be a part of His plan in bringing His message of forgiveness to our neighbors, friends, co-workers and the rest of the world. It is not His plan for us to sit at home or in a church and have a checklist of things to do each day to make us "spiritual." He desires His children to follow in His footsteps and reach others. We have gained salvation through faith in Christ, and we have the opportunity to offer others to do the same. Getting back to the heart of God is something we can't afford to pass up. Friend, don't let the list of "to do's" get in the way of living in the heartbeat of God. You can never do something for God that He can't do for Himself. All He desires of you is that you abide in His love, follow Him, and help spread His Gospel. Remember that obeying rules should be a *result* of your relationship with God, not the way to find Him.

"Pastor Steve, how do I know what God wants me to do with my life?" Tim asked.

Pastor Steve was pleased with Tim's question. "Well, Tim, first and foremost, He wants you to be changed into the likeness of Jesus. And after that, you need to seek His will for your life. Ask Him what His desire is for your life. And then wait for His response. But be prepared. He will show you what He wants and it may not be what you think!"

"What do you mean?" Tim exclaimed.

"Well, let me give you an example," Pastor Steve said. "When I was young, I wanted to be a doctor. I had always dreamed of saving someone's life on the operating table. It was a childhood dream that carried over to college. I went to school with that as my goal. But, when I started really searching out God's will, I felt Him specifically telling me that I was to be a pastor."

"Wow! How did He say that to you?" Tim cried.

Pastor Steve laughed. "Well, to be honest, I'm not exactly sure. Just over a period of time, I had a feeling about it that kept growing and getting stronger. Then things started to line up in my life. My interest in medicine declined. I was shown that being a doctor wasn't all glory and chivalry. It was a business, like any other—except the product to be sold is medicine. I turned to my pastor and asked him for advice. He asked me to pray every day for a month that God would show me exactly what I was to do with my life—for His glory, not mine. So I did. And at the end, I was so sure that I left that college and enrolled in seminary the next semester.

"But, Tim, you can serve Him in a whole variety of ways. We are all called to serve God with our lives, whatever our career. You can serve Him at your office right now by being a witness to His love and grace. The way you live your life speaks volumes to others. Then when you share the Gospel message with them, they will take note and listen. But again, first and foremost is your relationship with Him. He is more concerned with that than anything else. It is His joy to be in an intimate relationship with His children. That's His heart. Nothing else we do is as important as that."

Reflection

How is God calling you to get to the heart of the matter in your own life?

1.
2.
3.

What can hold you back from showing God's love to others?

1.
2.
3.

What does God's Word say about what holds you back?

1.
2.
3.

CHAPTER 5
STOP *GOING* TO CHURCH—START *BEING* THE CHURCH

That Sunday, Tim was greeted by Frank, a smiling older man at the church door who was greeting people as they walked up the steps, holding the door for all who entered. It was a blustery day. You could hear the snow and wind whipping through the trees and rushing into the small church every time the door was opened. Tim brushed off his snow-covered coat and said hello to his friends who he had gotten to know over the past several months. It was a slightly smaller crowd today, probably from the weather. Although the church was not full of people, you could feel that it was indeed full of the Spirit of God. As usual, after the worship team took their seats, Pastor Steve began his sermon.

"'...Upon this rock I will build my church and the gates of Hell will not withstand it,'" he said. A long pause followed as Pastor Steve looked around the church. "Matthew tells us that Jesus said this in the 18th verse of the 16th chapter" (KJV). Another long pause. "I want to look at this passage with you this morning. What exactly does He mean by this? First, we will look at what a church is. What is it that Jesus is building on the rock of faith? He has just asked the disciples who people say He is and gotten a variety of answers. Then He asked them who *they* say that He is. Peter answers with 'You are the Christ, the son of the living God'! This was a bold statement from Peter, who is rebuked by Jesus only five verses later when Jesus tells them that He must suffer and die. Peter argues with Him about having to suffer and is told, 'Get behind me, Satan! You are a stumbling block to me…' But here, Peter shows great faith, declaring that Jesus is the Messiah.

"I want to look at two things—what Jesus is building and where He is building it. First, what is He building? Well, the text tells us that He is building His church. So, what is a church? Is it a large building made of stone and colored glass? Is Jesus building a new and improved temple for us to worship in? Scripture tells us in Colossians, chapter 1, verse 24, that the church is the body of Christ. In Romans, chapter 12, verse 5 it says, '...in Christ, we who are many form one body....' In Ephesians, chapter 5, verse 30, we see that we are members of His body.

"According to J.C. Lambert, author of *Church,* the original Greek word used is *ekklesia*, which literally means 'called out.' In pre-Christian times, it was used to describe an assembly or a group of people 'called out' by the herald for the discussion and decision of public business.

"So, I want you to look at your idea of what 'church' means. What do you picture when I say 'church'? Many think of a building that has a tall steeple and stained glass windows. But that is not what the scripture teaches us. When the word 'church' is used in scripture, generally it is referring to a body, or group of believers. When Paul writes to the Corinthians and Thessalonians, he addresses his letters to the 'church' in those areas. I assure you he was not writing to a brick building! He was writing to a group of people who believed that Jesus is the Messiah, the promised Savior. Churches are not buildings, my friends! They are living bodies of people who profess faith in Christ.

"So many go *to* a church, week after week, checking it off their list of things to do, hoping to one day experience something. So many people go hoping to find God. And many stop going because they never do. They go *to* a church, go through the motions, looking for Christ to give them life and hope, never getting involved or really surrendering to the Lord. They go *to* a church to find God.

"Dear friends, we *are* the church. We are His body. He dwells in us, not a building. He came to save us and to live within us. He doesn't contain Himself in a building and wait for us to visit Him on a weekly basis. We are His temples. It has nothing to do with a building. How many times have you said to a friend, 'I'll see you at church'? Or told your kids, 'Come on, we're going to be late for church'? How can we be late for ourselves?

"Jesus said that where two or more are gathered, there He is in their midst. Where did we get the idea that we need to go somewhere to worship? The early church had no buildings to call their own. They met in homes or in the temple courts or wherever they could to share with one another and celebrate what Christ had done for them. I encourage you to take a good look at your understanding of what 'church' is all about and realize that we are the body of Christ—the church. He has no desire to build buildings as meeting places for people. Rather, He wants to use His church—you and me—to reach this world with the message of the gospel.

"So, now that we know *what* the church is, where is He building it? He is building His church in the hearts of believers around the world. He is building the church on the rock of faith. Faith in what He has done for us at the cross. Don't think about this building as the church. It is our church's building, but nothing more. It is the tool that we use to gather together and be strengthened in the word of God. Jesus tells us in Luke, chapter 21, verse 33 that 'heaven and earth will pass away, but my words will never pass away.' This building that you are in, the chair you are sitting in, this microphone, all of it is in the process of passing away. The only thing that will remain is His Word. Jesus said that He is building His church and the gates of Hell will not prevail against it. He speaks of an immortal church, one that will last for eternity. He is not speaking of bricks and mortar. He is speaking of you and me—our souls, being with Him in Heaven, forever praising and glorifying Him.

"God never desired us to live in a world like we do that is so far from the ideal that He has for us. Although He knew that the world would end up in the state it is in, His plan for the world was so different. His plan was the Garden of Eden, where man freely interacted with God, and He provided for every need. We were not designed to live in a sinful world. But by God's grace we are able to get strengthened so that we can.

"So what is our role as the church? We are called to do battle with Satan! We are called to bring the Gospel into all of the world so that the grace of God can go forth. We need to go forward in this world, as a light in the darkness. We need to bring the joy that we have to a hurting people. We need to overcome our fears and things that hold us back so we can become a tool for God. Then He can truly use us.

"His primary purpose or goal for us is to be conformed into the likeness of Christ. He has given all of us gifts that we need so that we can fulfill that purpose. Satan tries to stop that from happening. We need to pray and get it deep within ourselves that

'Greater is He that is in us than is in the world!' We can overcome Satan's attacks and be a warrior for God. Take some time and think about your role in the kingdom. What work does God have for you that you have not begun yet? I pray that you will ask Him for guidance and that He would show you your gift—your weapon of warfare that you can use to help build His church with Him."

On the way home Tim kept thinking about what Pastor Steve had said. *What is my weapon? How can God use me?* He hoped that God would show him his place in the body, where he could use his gift, whatever it happened to be. He was filled with excitement and fear at the same time. He wanted so much to know his part and to jump in, but the unknown was like a pool of wet cement that he was afraid he would slowly slip into. When he got home, he took out his planner and on the top of each page for the next forty days, he wrote in the task, 'Seek God's direction!' He made a commitment with himself to ask God about His plans for his life, just as Pastor Steve had done. He was determined to find out God's plan for his life and follow it, no matter what.

God is building His church—His body here on earth. And because of our faith in Christ, we are a part of that body. He desires us to be His church, His bride, His hands, His feet. We are to be a living example to the world of what Jesus did for them so they will desire to know Him the way we do. God's plan is to use His spirit, living within us to minister to others and to meet their needs. We have an incredible privilege of being called to be a part of God's work here on Earth. We all have a different purpose, just as a leg has a purpose and an arm has another. We have all been given different gifts that He wants us to use, so when we come together as one, we will complement one another and strengthen one another as we each do our work (Eph. 4:16).

What stops us from getting involved in His work? People today are busier than ever. They are busy with work, family, sports, kids, and life in general. We have become so busy with things to do that we have lost focus on what is important in life. One area I see this in is entertainment. We have become so focused on entertainment that we have become utterly useless for the Kingdom of God. That may sound pretty harsh. Let me explain.

Our focus as a society on sports and entertainment has become a kind of god to us. I don't mean that we sit in our homes and bow to our television sets, but anything that comes before God and His desire is a form of idolatry. There are people that I know who don't go to their church service if a big game is on TV. Likewise, many people who participate in sports leagues find themselves skipping worship and going to their games instead. They have more commitment to their team members than to God Himself.

Many churches offer their congregations alternate times to worship. On one hand, this is a nice gesture that attracts many to come; but are we giving the message that church is something that needs to be "checked off" on a weekly to-do list, or "gotten out of the way" so we can do what we want to do? What happened to making time for God? Is it that hard to sacrifice time and energy to worship Him, even if it is not convenient or does not fit into our carefully planned week? I believe that we need to get back to a true sense of worship in this country, putting Him first—before sports and clubs and even family. If that doesn't happen, I'm afraid He will remove His hand of blessing from our nation.

One reason I believe this happens is because of the priorities we hold as a culture. Men typically get satisfaction and fulfillment from doing something—working, building, etc. Many see Christianity as a spectator event where we spend an hour singing some songs, listening to someone read from Scripture, and then going home. With this mindset, there isn't a "place" for them to get involved—no task to accomplish. Even though this mentality couldn't be farther from the truth, it is a common complaint in churches today. There is a call to men today to get involved in their churches. Not just as chair-warmers, but as active members who are interested in reaching the lost around them, bringing more and more people into the fold of God.

Have you ever asked God what your mission is; why you are where you are; what He wants you to do with the gifts He has given you? I encourage you to spend the next fifteen to thirty minutes simply asking God what He wants from your life. Expect Him to answer. Then write down what you hear or feel the Lord is saying to you. He desires to have you fulfill your mission. He created you for a specific purpose, whether you want to believe it or not. He wants to tell you so you will find fulfillment in this life. Quiet your mind and wait for God's answer. You can use the space provided to write down what God reveals to you.

You will never be content and fulfilled until you are doing what you are called to do. For so many years, I would decide what I wanted to do and ask God to bless my decision, as if He had no say in my design. One day I decided to do it differently. I decided to seek God's direction for my life and follow His leading. Friend, it was an amazing time. Once you seek God's direction and follow His leading in your life, you will start to feel a sense of accomplishment and fulfillment. The things you have gone through will start to make sense, and you will see how He has orchestrated events to mold and shape you in the way you needed to be molded. He is using things in your life to make you into the person He wants you to be, to fulfill His plan for you.

Take that step of faith and seek His guidance. And then write it down! You will be so thankful in the future that you did. When things get hard, and they will, you will be able to reflect on what God said. It will motivate and encourage you when you want to give up. I pray that you will follow His leading. It will be a definite turning point in your life.

Reflection

As instructed, spend 15 minutes listening to what God wants for your life. Then write down what He says.

How do you sense God calling you to get more involved in His church? What is your specific role in the church, for which God has equipped you?

How can you better prepare and equip yourself for the role to which you have been called?

1.

2.

3.

How can you help others fulfill their roles?

1.

2.

3.

CHAPTER 6

GOING FISHING— WHAT'S ON *YOUR* HOOK?

As Tim pulled into the church parking lot, he glanced at the dashboard clock. 11:38! Once again he was running late. He had attempted to push "snooze," but instead had turned off his alarm. He slowly opened the old wooden church doors, trying not to let the squeak attract attention to his lateness. He slipped into the back row, which was empty, and began to listen. Pastor Steve had just begun his sermon for the morning. Tim had missed the praise songs that he had grown to love so much. He reached for a bulletin to find out what the topic was for that morning—Fishing. *This should be good*, he thought.

Pastor Steve began, "Most of us have heard that Jesus asked some of His disciples to follow Him and He would make them 'fishers of men.' These men were fishermen by trade. Their whole lives were tied up in their businesses. It was the only way they had to support themselves and their families. Yet they left it all behind to follow Jesus. Even though they may have known that Jesus was a prophet or a man of God, they had no idea where He would take them or if they would ever be back. In spite of this, they willingly laid down their nets, left their homes, their families, their businesses, and comforts to follow this man, Jesus.

"They didn't ask Him where they were going, what they were planning to do, when or if they would be back, or how far they would be traveling. They packed nothing and took no possessions with them. They simply dropped what they were doing and followed Jesus. They walked away from their security and families to follow a teacher who they had very limited information about. What would you have done if you were in their shoes? What would your response be today if Jesus asked you to follow Him like that?

"Maybe you never have thought about it before, but He is asking you the very same thing today. He desires you to be fishers of men. He wants each of you on His team. Jesus says to us in Mark 9:40, 'Whoever is not against us is for us.' There is no gray area. You are either on His team or you are the opponent. So what does being on the team really mean in our culture? How do we 'fish for men' in the 21st century?

"First let's take a look at regular fishing. In Jesus' day, the men He called used large nets to catch fish and pull them up into their boats. It was a hard, backbreaking job that didn't always yield the results that they desired. In Luke 5:4-9, we see that Peter and his companions, James and John, had fished all night but caught nothing. Jesus used this frustrating event to show His power when He commanded them to lower their nets again, and they pulled up a catch that almost broke their nets!

"Today, when we think of fishing, we usually think of using a pole, a hook, and bait. I want to use that picture of fishing to illustrate our calling to be fishers of men. As a boy, I went fishing with my father several times. We would go out after dark the night before and catch the worms we needed for bait. We would wake early the next morning and fish for hours, many times not catching more than two or three small sunfish. Even though we wouldn't catch many fish, we would still go through a good number of worms in the process. The worms acted as an attraction for the fish. If you've ever been fishing, you know that putting an empty hook in the water isn't the most productive method. The fish aren't attracted to the hook, but to what's on the hook.

"So what's on *your* hook? When we are fishing for men, what do we have that attracts others and makes them want what we have? What are you offering that will make them stop swimming around lost in this world and start to pursue God? It's a delicate matter to consider, my friends. You don't want to water down Christianity just to make it appealing, but your life—your walk with Christ—should have something that they don't have—a light, a purpose, a peace based on your relationship with the Creator.

"Look at the message of the Gospel as your spiritual hook. Don't think you have to water it down or sweeten the deal! It couldn't get any better than it already is. You have eternal life based on your acceptance of Jesus' work on the cross. It's not about following rules and regulations, a set of dos and don'ts, or any of those things that people get so caught up in. When people look at your life, they will see that you are different. You should have the peace of Christ, the peace they are looking for. It is the worm, the bait—their desire. They will want to know what your 'secret' is.

"The door will be open for you to share the greatest story ever told. You can share with them and invite them to ask Jesus into their life, right there. It doesn't matter where you are. You don't have to make a special appointment or anything. Just share from your heart about the change He has made in your life, explain the plan that God has for them, and sit back and watch the Spirit convict them. But just like in fishing, you will get several 'bites' that don't result in a catch. Just like Jesus explained in the parable of the sower, not all of your seeds will end up in fertile ground.

"Be careful, my dear friends, that you don't try to fish only through your life and actions. Being an evangelist doesn't just mean living a life that reflects Christ and never talking to people about why you are living your life the way you are. You need to have a verbal explanation ready of what you believe and why, so you can let others know about the most important part of your life—your relationship with the God of the universe—and how they can share the same intimacy that you do.

"Like I said, it's a delicate balance of living out your faith and sharing it with others. If your life isn't showing the fruit of you being a disciple of Jesus, it doesn't matter how much you preach to your friends and co-workers, or how suave you are when you explain things to people. They will see through your act. You need to live what you preach and preach what you live. That is our part in fishing for men. The rest is up to God to catch their heart with His hook and reel them into a loving relationship with Himself. We can cast out our line, but the great fisherman in the sky reels them in!

"I pray that each of us takes a look at our own life and evaluates ourselves. Are there some things in your life now that would prevent others from trusting your presentation of the Gospel? Are you living what you say and saying what you believe about Jesus? I encourage each of you to go before the Lord and ask Him to reveal areas in your life that are hindering your fishing. Ask Him to show them to you and help to fix them so that He can use you to fish for men."

Tim sat in his seat and thought about his life. *Was he living as a disciple? Did others see anything in his life like Pastor Steve was talking about?* Tim made a commitment that he would do everything he could to change so that he could be a fisher of men.

After the service, he was getting some coffee in the fellowship hall and noticed Pastor Steve walking toward him. "That was a really great sermon, Pastor. I enjoyed it a lot."

"Well, Tim, I'm glad that you liked it. And I'm so glad you're here. I was worried when I didn't see you this morning. Is everything okay?"

"Yes, I just overslept a little."

"Well, I'm glad that you made it. I want to introduce you to someone."

As he followed Pastor Steve, Tim noticed they were walking toward a gray-haired Indian couple that was surrounded by twenty or thirty people from the church. "Who are they?" he asked.

"They are true fishers of men. I've known them for about 30 years. They have been great friends and an encouragement to me as I felt God leading me into ministry. Pastor Keith is a missionary and pastor of a small church in western India. They have spoken here several times about their ministry. I want you to meet them. I think you'd like their story."

"Pastor Keith?" Tim asked. "That doesn't sound very Indian."

"You're right," Pastor Steve explained. "His real name is Subramanian, but he goes by Keith when he is here in the U.S. It's a lot easier for us to say!"

"Pastor Keith, this is Tim Riley. I wanted you to meet him. He's one of our newest members God has blessed us with."

"Nice to meet you, Tim," Pastor Keith said in a thick accent, as he shook Tim's hand.

"Nice to meet you also. I hear that you are a pastor in India. That must be exciting."

"Well, Tim," Pastor Keith replied, "it is always very exciting when you follow God. What about you? What do you do?"

"I work at a law firm." Tim replied with a smile.

"Forgive me, Tim, but I thought your job is to be a fisherman, isn't it? Isn't that what Pastor Steve just told you?"

"Well, I guess you're right. I'll have to remember that." As they talked for the next few minutes, Tim felt as if they had made an instant connection somehow.

As they parted, Pastor Keith said, "I hope we can meet again sometime soon. I would like it if you could come to India and fish with me."

Do you have bait on your hook? Do people around you at work, or even your family and friends see something in you that they can't quite figure out? Do they see the peace of God during the trials of life? Do they see His love and compassion shining through you? Unless we live out our faith and share the light of Christ with those we come into contact with, we are fooling ourselves.

Do you remember the story of the Good Samaritan? Be careful not to be like the Levite and the Priest who both knew the law of God but did not stop on the road to help the man in need. They decided not to live out their faith. We should try to live and act in a way that will make people see that God's peace and love are real, tangible things. In this way, when we talk to them about what Jesus has done for us, they will have already been shown a witness to the truth through our actions. They will not be able to deny that His grace is real. They would have already seen it in action through you. Bait your hook and GO FISHING! You'll be amazed at the catch that God will bring to your hook!

Reflection

What are some ways that you can be more involved in "fishing for men" right where you are?

1.

2.

3.

What are some things that hinder you from getting more involved in reaching out to people around you?

1.

2.

3.

How can you grow past those obstacles and step out in faith to share with others?

1.

2.

3.

CHAPTER 7
BEING REAL, NOT RELIGIOUS

"It sure is a slow ride today due to the snow," Tim heard the morning news reporter say as he lay in bed after his alarm went off. *Snow! What snow?* He rolled out of bed and looked out his window to see a thick white blanket on everything, including his car. It had been a beautiful day yesterday, sunny and in the forties. He had gone to bed early last night and hadn't heard the weather report. *I better hurry up so I have time to brush off my car,* he thought.

As he was outside scraping the layer of snow and ice from his windshield, he saw his neighbor, an older woman, struggling with her car. It seemed that she couldn't find the snowbrush and was trying to use a kitchen spatula to get the ice and snow off.

"Can I help you with that?" Tim called to her.

"That would be wonderful," the woman responded. "I thought I would be out here all day!"

After introductions as Tim began to work on her windshield, he remembered what Pastor Steve had said about "fishing." *What can I do to bring up God to her?* he wondered. She asked him where he worked, trying to make small talk while he scraped the ice off. Here was his chance!

"I work at Jefferson and Associates on East Main Street. It's right down the street from the little white church on the corner."

"Oh! I know right where that is."

"Do you go to that church?" Tim asked, knowing she didn't.

"No. I don't...well...I used to go to church," she replied. "Not anymore...ever since my boy died." She paused and tears welled up in her eyes. "It's complicated." She smiled and stepped away to the other side of the car.

"I'm sorry to hear about your son," Tim replied, feeling bad about bringing up a painful memory. "Your car is all set. Be careful driving this morning, Alice. It was nice to meet you."

"Thank you so much. I would have been here for a long time without your help."

How many times have you heard someone say, "I don't want anything to do with God," "I don't need your rules," "I don't need to go to church," or "Christians aren't any better than me!"? What are they really saying? They have been hurt. Maybe they had attended church but someone offended them. Maybe they had something happen to them and blame God for it. They may have seen something at a church that they didn't like. Or they may have seen unconfessed sin in someone who professed to be a believer. Whatever actually happened, they now have a distorted view of what being a Christian is and want nothing to do with God, as in the case of Tim's neighbor, Alice. What a crime!—to act in a way that makes a potential brother stumble. It is a terrible thing that we all should guard against.

I once heard someone share that because her son was going through trouble, other parents in her church told their kids to avoid contact with him. Is that truly the Christian attitude we should have? Certainly they are trying to protect their kids from getting involved with "the wrong crowd," but what about the body coming together and helping each other through difficult times? Why not come to his aid, show him the love of Christ, and build up his trust in God during the trouble? Now he may think that because he did something wrong, he is being rejected by the church family. And if the church is rejecting him, he probably thinks God is as well. See the cycle we start without even knowing it? We are called to be witnesses for Christ, not prosecutors for Christ!

After the tragedy of September 11th, people around the country came to church services and vigils. A renewed interest in God awoke throughout our nation. You couldn't go anywhere without seeing a flag or bumper sticker that said "God Bless America!" But within months, things were back to "normal." Church attendance shrunk. People's interest in God shifted to other things. The California court said that it was unconstitutional to use "God" in the Pledge of Allegiance. Why? Why did we see so many people come to churches around the country and then in unison, as if being directed, leave to go back to their God-less lives?

Did they come to a church in *your* town? Did they come back to God, seeking Him to help them in their time of need? Why didn't they stay? Could it be that they didn't find what they came for? Could it be that they came to a church building, looking for God, and found just that—a building made of stone, brick, glass and wood? That's not what they came to find. They came to a church building to find God and if they had found Him—truly found HIM living in the people there—they would have stayed. They would have found a loving, just God who deeply cares about them—a God who went to the cross to buy for them the right to be called children of God. What *did* they find? Did they find politics, doctrine, and dos and don'ts? Did they find a community of believers that would drop whatever they were doing to aid someone in need, or a gathering of people with schedules so full that outreach didn't fit?

What an opportunity we had to drastically change the hearts and minds of people around this country. People who had turned from God, going on their own path, briefly came back to Him for healing in their time of need. Consider that there likely will be times in the future when people will come again to God. They will come to Him as a last hope—a last resort—when they don't know what else to do. We need to be prepared for them. We need to have compassion on them, just as Jesus does. We need to say no to soccer practice, golf, television, and anything else that interferes. We need to lay down our own lives for others, just as Christ laid down His life for us.

September 11th was a terrible tragedy. There is no question about that. But there are tragedies every day that happen in the lives of neighbors. At the times in people's lives when they are at their limit, they are often more open to God than at other times. The church needs to be ready and available. That is what Jesus wants. He can work miracles through us if we allow Him. We can see lives changed for the better every day—not just when disaster strikes.

Are we ready as a church body to jump in and save those drowning around us? Years ago, there was a less hectic pace in our society. People met with each other more often, sharing the ups and downs of life, helping each other through, lifting each other up. Over the years, that has gone by the wayside. We have replaced friends and neighbors with other activities. These activities often alienate us and make strangers out of our neighbors. I remember when my wife and I first moved to Orlando, we knew one couple in our apartment complex well enough to call them friends. We saw several people who lived around us briefly, just long enough to say "hi" in the morning or evening. They were simply acquaintances. There were hundreds of people who lived there, but because our culture doesn't value getting to know new people, we were strangers to almost everyone we saw.

If our neighbors were in need, sadly, we would not have known. If they were going through trials and were at the end of their rope, desperately needing to talk to someone, we would not have known. This is sad! Think about the people who live near you. How many of them are true neighbors—ones that you know well and would know if they were in need? How many are merely acquaintances?

In Luke 10:37, Jesus told us to "... 'love your neighbor as yourself.'" How are we doing? Are we passing this test? He didn't simply mean our fellow brothers and sisters at church. To illustrate the point, He shared the story of the Good Samaritan, a stranger from another town taking care of a man who was beaten and robbed. We are called to be everyone's neighbor. We are called to be Jesus' body to the whole world. That is what being real is about!

Jesus met the real needs of people around Him. He gave sight to the blind, healed diseases, allowed the deaf to hear, and fed those who followed Him. He was interested in their physical well-being as well as their spiritual life. We too need to be interested in our neighbors' physical needs. When we find a balance between meeting physical and spiritual needs, we find that our lives are full of blessing. When we stop being religious and start being real with one another and our neighbors, people start to see what God is all about. If we stay in our boxes—our church buildings, homes and church programs—we will not be able to show Christ's love to the world around us. We could have the entire Bible memorized, but if people around us don't see Jesus and feel His love in our actions, we are useless to the Kingdom.

The Pharisees were very knowledgeable about scriptures. They quoted it to Jesus several times, trying to point out that Jesus was not following their interpretation. Each time, Jesus showed them that they knew the words, but missed the heartbeat. They were consumed with following laws and rules to the tee, but were ignorant of God's intent for the Law. They were knowledgeable about the Law but ignorant of love, on which the Law is based (Matt. 22:36-40). We need to be careful that we don't turn into modern-day Pharisees. We need to keep Jesus' teaching real in our life, not just on pages of scripture. We need to live them out and truly be salt and light to the dark world we live in. Then we will be able to more fully understand them and appreciate the amazing love that God has bestowed on us.

How do we keep His teachings real in our life? We must start by caring for and loving people. Not a "love" that the world has to offer, but deep, true love for one another. Jesus told us that the greatest commandment is to love God with all our heart, mind, soul and strength. He said the second is like it—to love our neighbor as ourselves! You may say, "I know a lot of people who love their friends and family and are not believers." There is a difference between the type of love that the world gives and the type Jesus is talking about here. Jesus said that the world would know that we are His disciples because of the love we show others! Jesus was speaking about an unconditional, sacrificial love based on nothing less than the love that God has already shown us. We cannot use anything else as our measure for love. No matter how much we may love others, when we compare it to the vast, limitless love of God, it pales in comparison.

To be an example of love in the world—to demonstrate a small glimpse of God's love—we must not just know about what Jesus did and said. We must daily live out His words and His actions in our own life. When we begin to put ourselves aside and stop taking care of our own needs first, we become a living example of God's mercy and love to others. And the amazing thing is that when we do this, God Himself will fill us with everything we need. When we take care of others and live for Him, He takes care of us and lives through us!

Think about something you can do that would show God's love to others around you. It may be giving food to a food pantry or church, or going to a neighbor who is hurting and inviting them to have coffee with you, building a relationship with them over time and being a source of comfort to them. It may be inviting a family in your neighborhood to attend church with you or having a garage sale and donating all of the proceeds to someone who lost their house due to a fire. You could make a meal for someone who lost their job and is struggling, and just leave it on their front porch with a note "God loves you." What the action is doesn't matter. But start to think about things you can do to meet physical needs of people around you while reaching out to their spiritual needs with God's love.

Step back and evaluate your life. Seek God's direction and you will begin to devote yourself to being *real*, not religious!

Reflection

What are some behaviors or habits that you have seen in members of the church that are offensive to you and could be offensive to others?

1.
2.
3.

Have you caught yourself acting in these ways? If so, please describe.

1.
2.
3.

How can you avoid losing focus on Jesus Christ in your life so you can live in a way that you are a constant reminder of God's love to others?

1.
2.
3.

CHAPTER 8
OBEYING JESUS' COMMANDS—WHAT DID JESUS SAY?

The following Sunday, Tim sat for a few minutes in the pew and thought about Pastor Steve's sermons over the last few weeks. He wondered if he was being religious or if he was trying to be real with others and with the Lord. *How do people see me?* he wondered. *What impact am I making? Am I a part of building the church?*

He asked Pastor Steve to go to lunch with him after he finished up with his Sunday routine. They shuffled off to a local diner to get lunch and enjoy each other's company. It had been a while. Tim's job was beginning to pick up and he had less time to stop by for conversations during the week.

A lady greeted them as they pushed the door open. "Hi, Judy!" exclaimed Pastor Steve. Tim smiled and nodded to the middle-aged woman wearing one of the biggest, warmest smiles he had ever seen.

"Hi,// Pastor. How was church today?" she asked.

"It was great. I wish you were there," Pastor Steve replied.

"Someday. Someday, I'll make it over to see you," she responded as she grabbed two menus and walked them toward an empty booth.

Once they had ordered, Pastor Steve asked Tim, "So what's new? How is the job going?"

"It's fine. I'm getting busy. I'm starting to pick up some extra work that my boss is giving me. They seem to like what I'm doing. I hope I can move up and make a name for myself."

"You have a great name already," Pastor Steve interjected and smiled. "It's written in His book."

"I know," Tim replied. "You know what I mean."

"I do. So, to what do I owe this honor? Why the lunch date? Is something on your mind?"

Smiling, Tim began, "Actually, there is. I got thinking about your sermon about being real. I wanted to find out more about that. How do I know that I'm being real and not just going through the motions, being religious?"

"That's a great question, Tim. Let me tell you a story. You see, several years ago, there was a wonderful campaign that attempted to get people thinking about their daily actions. It was called 'What would Jesus do?' If you looked for it, you saw 'WWJD' everywhere, on signs, bracelets, bumper stickers and all sorts of other merchandise. The question was simple, yet profound. How does your life stack up to the life that Jesus lived and wants you to be living? I saw it on Bible covers, pens, T-shirts, and coffee mugs. It was an encouraging message that made a lot of people take time out of their busy lives and think about the path that they were on."

"Yeah, I remember that," replied Tim, as Judy handed him his plate.

"Tim, that's what being real is all about. So many times we hear stories from scripture and we think to ourselves 'That's a nice story,' or 'That would be nice to do.' When that is our response, we are missing the point. The stories and teachings of scripture are intended for nothing less than to mold us into the image and likeness of Christ. Look at the teachings and commands of Jesus, and evaluate your own life based on nothing more than His words and desire for your life. Jesus said, 'Heaven and earth will pass away, but my words will never pass away' (Luke 21:33). His words are powerful. He has left us with His words in the Bible to be our guide.

"Don't make the mistake of thinking that just because something happened a long time ago, it can't teach you something. I think the best lessons learned are ones learned by someone else's mistakes. It saves you a lot of headaches that way."

Tim thought and replied, "So I need to look at the life of Jesus and see how mine stacks up against it?"

"Not just that," continued Pastor Steve, "but figure out how He would handle every situation that you're presented with and actually live out your life in the way that He would. Be loving and real with people, not judgmental. Be truly obedient to His Word. Have faith that He will fulfill His promises. And share your faith with others. By actually following His teachings, you will be transformed into His image. Then you will be living a life built on Him, not some rules. You will truly have His life in you, flowing out to others. That's being real."

Below are several passages from scripture that give a teaching or command from Jesus in five major areas: Love, Obedience, Faith, Being an example of Christ, and Sharing your faith with others. At the end of each section, take time to reflect and answer the questions that are provided. Write down a way to fulfill the teachings in your own life, making them part of your life and daily routine. Keep a journal of how your own life is impacted by keeping Jesus' commands. It may be helpful to do this with someone you trust, like a member of your Bible study, so that you have someone that you can be accountable to for any changes that you sense the Lord leading you to make.

Love—sharing it with the world

"...Love your enemies and pray for those who persecute you...." – Matt. 5:44

"... 'Love your neighbor as yourself'" – Matt. 19:19

"By this all men will know that you are my disciples, if you love one another" – John 13:35

Love is the thread that ties the entire Bible together into one expression of God. As followers of Christ, we experienced a sampling of the great, limitless love that Jesus had when He took our sins and paid our penalty for us. His love is far greater than we could ever hope to imagine. As Jesus' disciples, He calls us to share in the revelation of His love to the world. We are called to be messengers of the Gospel to all nations. Since the foundation of the Gospel message is love, we are also called to show His love to all nations!

We can start doing this, just as the early disciples did, in their hometown—Jerusalem. We can start showing Jesus' love to those who are in our Jerusalem—our neighborhood. Jesus desires us to not only "get along with" or "tolerate" others around us, but to truly love them, even when we disagree. Jesus sent His disciples out to preach the Gospel to a town that had just executed Him. They were commanded to preach and love the people, bringing with them the message of God's love and salvation. If we are to be His disciples, we need to do the same! We need to bring the love of Christ to those around us.

Year after year we feel compelled to be generous and to give around the holidays. We give to the Salvation Army at the malls, donate toys for children in need, bring canned goods to a local food pantry and so on. But what are we doing in March or August? We aren't called to be generous and loving only at certain times of the year. We are called to be generous and loving—period. So, what are some ways we can do that in our lives? Take a minute. Think about ways you can fulfill your calling to share God's love with those around you in each of the areas listed below.

- Bringing God's love to the poor and needy in your community.
- Being a loving friend to those who are lonely or depressed. A great place to start is a local nursing home.
- Ensuring that your neighbors know what God's love has done for them.
- Sharing Christ's love with your co-workers.

Obedience—being a true follower of Christ

"Why do you call me 'Lord, Lord' and do not do what I say?"
– Luke 6:46

"If you love me, you will obey what I command."
– John 14:15

"My sheep hear my voice, and I know them, and they follow me; and I give eternal life to them, and they will never perish; and no one will snatch them out of my hand." – John 10:27-28 NASB

"Then he said to them all: 'If anyone would come after me, he must deny himself and take up his cross daily and follow me. For whoever wants to save his life will lose it, but whoever loses his life for me will save it.'" – Luke 9:23-24

"...Any of you who does not give up everything he has cannot be my disciple." – Luke 14:33

Even though we know that God sees all our actions and hears all our thoughts, we somehow deceive ourselves thinking that we can separate areas of our life from His view and keep them hidden from Him. We try to separate our "personal" life from our "spiritual" life. We attempt to be "spiritual" on Sundays and to completely ignore the leading that He gives us on a daily basis. We need to realize that Jesus is not looking for a certain percentage of our life. He is looking for ALL of our life. Paul says that he had to "die daily" to follow Christ.

To really experience His power in our life, we have to get out of the way! We cannot hold onto a part of our old life and fully experience the new life He desires us to have. The old life must be done away with. We must fully surrender our will to Him, making our priorities His priorities, making our will His will. Then we will see His hand on our life in a powerful way. We will bear fruit and be used by Him to touch others. We will truly be His disciples.

Are you willing to let Jesus be the true Lord of your life and obey His leading in every area of your life?

Are you willing to give up career, friends, habits and desires to follow His leading?

Do you trust Him to never lead you down a wrong path?

Are there habits in your life that you are not yet willing to let go of that are in contradiction to the teachings of the Bible; for example, lying, stealing, etc.?

Are there things in your life that you sense God asking you to do without?

Are there things that the Bible teaches that you should be doing that you are currently unwilling to do? Perhaps it's fellowshipping on a regular basis with a local church, giving financially to God's work, etc.

When you hear God guiding you to do something, what is your typical response?

Are you open and excited about hearing from God, or do you disregard what you hear Him say and continue on your own path?

Is it easier for you to give up material things than your own plans and your own will for your life? Why?

Having Faith

"...your faith has healed you." – Matt. 9:22

"Everything is possible for him who believes." – Mark 9:23

"If you believe, you will receive whatever you ask for in prayer." – Matt. 21:22

Many times when people would come to Jesus and ask to be healed, He would heal them and tell them that it was their faith that made them well (Matt. 9:29, Mark 10:52, Luke 17:19). He was teaching a principle that we find throughout scripture. God works through our faith in Him. In Mark 5:25-34 we find the story of a sick woman. She had so much faith that she thought if she could just touch Jesus' garment, He would heal her. She had such faith in Jesus' power to heal that she believed He would heal her without even directly asking Him! As soon as she touched the robe Jesus was wearing, His healing power entered her and cured her illness.

In contrast, once when Jesus was with His disciples on a boat, a violent storm came upon the lake. They panicked, and woke Him up saying, "...don't you care if we drown?" (Mark 4:38). He rebuked the storm, and then rebuked His disciples for their lack of faith. They were sitting next to the Creator of the universe, yet were afraid that they would perish because of a storm. This is how we live many times in our walk with God. We have the very Spirit of God dwelling within us, yet we get anxious and afraid of something that is happening in our lives. We forget that the Creator is with us. If He desired, you would not have this challenge in your life to begin with. He allowed it into your life to fulfill His purposes, not yours.

We often think that He has forgotten us when bad things happen in our lives. That could not be farther from the truth. He allows experiences, even ones we consider "bad experiences," to help us become who He wants us to be. If we have faith that God loves us and has allowed things for a reason, our faith will be stretched and become stronger. In such times, being in fellowship will greatly help us in our walk. When we are going through a time when things seem dark and grim, we need to rely on other brothers and sisters to keep a good perspective. We need others to help us understand what God is doing in our lives through the events we are struggling through.

Times in our lives that God intends for growth, Satan uses to rock the very foundation of our faith. Satan wants us to doubt and question God's sovereignty and His love for us. We need to have faith that God truly loves us and would never harm us.

Describe a time in your life that your faith has been tested.

Did you ever feel that God had abandoned or forgotten about you?

Looking back, can you see how God used it for good?

How did your faith grow as a result of that situation? Have you been able to help others who have gone through a similar situation?

Being an example of Christ's love and forgiveness

"You are the light of the world…let your light shine before men, that they may see your good deeds and praise your Father in heaven." – Matt. 5:14-16

"If someone strikes you on the right cheek, turn to him the other also. And if someone wants to sue you and take your tunic, let him have your cloak as well. If someone forces you to go one mile, go with him two miles." – Matt. 5:39b-41

"But I tell you: Love your enemies and pray for those who persecute you, that you may be sons of your Father in heaven...." – Matt. 5:44-45

Through the examples above, Jesus tells us that He desires our behavior to flow from our knowledge of Him, not our own desires or instincts. When we function as He wants us to, our lives look radically different from the status quo. We have a responsibility and calling to be a light to the world. But being a light isn't always an easy thing to do in a dark world. There are times when the world tries to snuff out our light so they don't have to see it. God uses it to convict them of things in their own life that are not up to the standard He has set. They want nothing more than to remove any standard that shows that they don't measure up. Living as a light requires faith and courage.

We cannot do it alone. It is completely against our human nature to follow Jesus' teachings. To turn and offer our other cheek to someone who has just slapped us is not the response that immediately comes to our minds. Praying for those who persecute us takes great faith. Our human spirit wants nothing to do with those who are enemies to us. We desire to be separated from our enemies, not to pray for them or forgive them or draw them into a relationship. But that is exactly what God has done with each of us. Romans 5:8 tells us that while we were still sinners, or enemies of God, Christ died for us, healing our broken relationship with Him. In the same way, He desires that we also forgive and rebuild our own broken relationships. By doing this, we will be showing the world one of the greatest examples of God's love.

Are there people in your life who have hurt you that you have never forgiven?

Are there people that you have hurt from whom you need to ask forgiveness?

What other way can you show your "enemies" God's love?

What are some ways that you have been shown God's love by those who you do not know well?

When you hold a grudge or unforgiveness, you are the one who ends up being in the bondage of that unforgiving spirit. Make a commitment to forgive people this week. The freedom that you will experience is unimaginable.

Sharing your faith with others

"Come, follow me, ...and I will make you fishers of men." – Matt. 4:19

"I am sending you out like sheep among wolves. Therefore be as shrewd as snakes and as innocent as doves." – Matt. 10:16

"No one who puts his hand to the plow and looks back is fit for service in the kingdom of God." – Luke 9:62

Jesus called His first disciples by inviting them to become fishers of men. After 2000 years, His invitation to us remains the same. We have been called to work side by side with Jesus in bringing the message of the Gospel to others. No matter what your profession, your primary job assignment is to bear witness for the Gospel to everyone you meet. Sharing the message is not reserved for a few select messengers, but is a task given to all of us. There is a wide variety of ways you can bear witness to Jesus' message. The method doesn't matter as much as the desire to see that others have the chance to know and experience God's forgiveness in their lives.

You are not just merely invited to participate, but rather are commanded to participate in His work. In Matthew 28:19-20, Jesus tells us to go and make disciples of all nations.... You are invited to become a part of the process, and in turn will be blessed for your efforts. So why is it that so many believers never talk about their beliefs with strangers, never sharing with them the message of the Gospel? You have a great gift to share with others. It is a gift that was freely offered to you and changed your life. Why would you not want to do the same for someone else who desperately needs to hear about Jesus? There will be times of rejection and fear. There will also be times of great joy as you lead someone in a prayer that literally saves their life! We are told so often from Satan about the rejection that we forget the reality of joy that is awaiting us!

Jesus said that He is sending us out as sheep among wolves. We need to be ready with the armor of God! We can put on His armor and be strengthened so that we will be ready when the battles come. He also warned us not to look back. Don't look back at the comfort that the world offers and turn down the joy that awaits you. You are called to become a part of the process. Fulfilling your calling will bring immeasurable satisfaction to your life.

What are some factors that stop you from sharing your faith with strangers?

How can you overcome these factors and be freed from them? Do you need training or encouragement from others?

Make a commitment to talk to someone about your faith this week. Simply starting a conversation about God's plan for your life with someone will plant seeds that can be watered in the future. Don't consider witnessing a success only when someone makes a decision for Christ. Every seed that is planted is a success that God will water and grow.

I pray that you will meditate on the commands that Jesus gave us. I hope that His words will penetrate your heart and that the desire to live out His commands will grow in your heart. To truly live out our faith takes work. It is not an easy life. Many times He warned his disciples that the road ahead of them would be hard, but the reward for their diligence would be more than worth it. I pray that you would continue to grow closer to Him as you walk the walk of faith, as you truly live out His commands, not just read about them. Make them part of your daily life. Do what Jesus said and you will surely have what Jesus promised!

Reflection

What stands between you and fully living out Jesus' commands?

1.
2.
3.

Which commands are the hardest for you to follow?

1.
2.
3.

Why do you struggle with those particular commands?

1.
2.
3.

CHAPTER 9
THE TRUTH, THE WHOLE TRUTH AND NOTHING BUT THE TRUTH

"Well, I used to go to church as a kid, but I stopped when I got older. I guess I can't buy all the stuff they teach."

"Like what?" Tim asked. Using some "bait" on his "hook," Tim had started a conversation about God with his co-worker, Larry, in the lunch room.

"Well," Larry continued, "like streets that are actually paved with gold in Heaven, that eating an apple started all the sin in the world, or that God really wants us to send all of our money to evangelists on TV. Don't get me wrong, there are a lot of nice things they teach at church, but I just can't believe everything they say. So I stopped going. I still believe in God and we take the kids on Christmas, but that's about it."

"So do you think that God created the world?" Tim asked.

"Well, I think He had something to do with it. Like maybe He made some stuff in space, or even the earth and other planets and they evolved into the form they're in today. Like us, He may have made life, but it evolved into human form. It makes more sense that way. There is so much proof of evolution. It had to happen that way."

"Interesting. I never heard that take on it before," Tim replied.

"Well, don't quote me on it," Larry continued. "It's just what I've come up with. What about you? How do you think we got here?"

"Well," Tim replied, "even though I may not understand how it all happened, I believe that the Bible is true. And I guess my stand is that whether I believe in something or not doesn't change the fact that it is true. Like gravity—if I stop believing in it, it doesn't make it untrue. All that changes is my belief. I think it's the same way with God. When we don't understand or believe something in the Bible, it still remains true."

"Well, I can't buy some of it. You're a better man than me," answered Larry.

"Not at all, I just believe that God's word is true and real—period. Listen, I have to get to a meeting. We should pick this up again sometime," concluded Tim.

"That sounds good. I'll see you later."

Like Larry, everyone has their own opinion about God and His role in their life. The truth is that God created us to be in fellowship with Him and has given us a built-in desire to worship Him. In Ephesians 3:17, Paul tells us that Jesus will "dwell in your hearts by faith." There is an empty space within our spirit that is built for Jesus to fill. When we accept His gift of salvation, His spirit comes to live with us and strengthen us. A popular song's lyrics say that we have a "God-shaped hole in our heart."

But what happens when we don't have God's spirit within us? Does that space simply remain empty? Sometimes we are filled with a spirit that does not come from God. The Bible talks about a "spirit of timidity" (2 Tim. 1:7). Jesus tells us in Luke 11:24 that when someone has an evil spirit that is cast out, unreplaced by God's Spirit, it will go and bring other spirits with itself back to that person so the person's state is worse than it was originally.

Because of this innate desire to worship and be filled spiritually, we find ourselves in a world where people have created other gods to worship. Because they do not know the living, true God yet have a built-in desire to worship, they create a vast array of idols. In India, for example, where Hinduism is the prominent religion, there are over 250,000,000 gods and goddesses to worship, each believed to be an attribute of a god that you will never fully know. Some cultures worship the earth itself, as the supplier of life. In doing so, they fail to recognize that God created and gave the earth to us and provides for us through the earth. They mistake the gift for the giver. Psalm 115:2-8 speaks of those who do not know God but instead worship idols:

> Why do the Nations say, "Where is their God?" Our God is in Heaven; He does whatever pleases Him. But their idols are silver and gold, made by the hands of men. They have mouths, but cannot speak, eyes, but they cannot see; they have ears but cannot hear, noses but they cannot smell; they have hands but cannot feel, feet but they cannot walk; nor can they utter a sound with their throats. Those who make them will be like them, and so will all who trust in them.

Those are obvious examples of people creating a god to follow. Many times we look at others in our own culture and see that their lives and actions are not in line with God's plan. We usually don't think about them being idol worshippers. Many times we look at them as non-believers and nothing more. But what is a non-believer? I don't think that people can truly be non-worshippers. They will find something to worship—something to base their actions and decisions on. They will form a driving belief in their life, a goal to reach, a crusade to lead, a cause to support—something that gives them meaning and purpose. They may disagree with me, but they are not giving their time, energy, and passion to something just because they have nothing better to do. They believe in the causes they fight for. They believe that if they accomplish their mission, that they or others will benefit in some way. They look to these things to find fulfillment and justification.

There is nothing wrong with wanting to make the world a better place or fighting for a cause. But when the cause is the focus, we dethrone God from our life and replace Him with our cause. As we saw in chapter 3, worship is designed to bring glory and honor to the object of our worship. When we shift the focus and redirect glory from God to our mission or our work, we are in the act of worshipping that action. We cannot serve two masters (Matt. 6:24). We cannot worship God and separately follow our cause. We need to follow God Himself and His plan for our lives.

Another example of this is how we treat the great freedom that has been given to us in this country. At the expense of many lives, we have an unprecedented amount of freedom. We have been blessed. But what has happened over the past few decades? We have seen our "freedom" used to push God out of our society and to declare that we can make up our own set of moral laws.

We act as if we are not under any kind of law other than our own whims.

We use our "freedom" to justify our actions when they contradict not only God's law, but the conscience of people. We see people being arrested for leaving a dog in a car too long in the summer (which I am in no way condoning), but we are free to have abortions whenever we want to. We see young girls giving birth to children and putting them in garbage cans because they have no way of taking care of them. Everyone is horrified at this and it makes the news. But how can we be surprised at their actions when we have told them for so long that unborn babies are not humans and have no rights?

Our freedom is a precious thing, but over the years we have begun to worship the gift instead of the giver. We have elevated our gift of freedom to a place in our lives that we are willing to defend it to the death and will stop at nothing to protect it. But we have turned our back on the One who gave us the freedom. Many do not even acknowledge His existence; but for those who do, they tell Him that America does not need Him. They believe that we are self-sufficient and smart enough that we do not need the wisdom found in His book. We have elevated ourselves to be in God's position, making decisions on what is right and wrong based on our desires. It is a dangerous place to be in. Our pride has swelled in this country to a place of godlessness.

So what is our role as the church in this? First, we need to be very careful that we are not doing the same thing within our own lives. We so often have wonderful programs and outreaches designed to bring people closer to God that at some point we lose our original focus. We begin, gradually, to focus on the project and results instead of God. We cannot reach others with God's love if we are worshipping our work! Our work within the church needs to always be treated as an *assignment* from the Master, not *as* our master. God needs to remain the center of our lives and ministries so He can work through us.

We can be just as guilty of idolatry as the pagans in scripture, worshipping stone gods. We need to guard against this so that glory will be brought to God, not ourselves through our work. Once we ensure that our worship is pure, we can reach out to others around us. We need to convey that even if they don't think of actions as worship, they actually are. They need to know that their intent to live their life their own way is actually an act of self-worship. Chasing materialism and power is idolatry. Denying God's existence is also an act of worshipping ourselves or nature as the provider of life. They need to see the truth so they can worship the Truth, which is Jesus.

Many who profess to be believers are only fooling themselves with these types of issues. Truth cannot be partial truth. It has to be completely truthful or it is not truth at all. Faith can't be tailor-made for each person. Truth is universal, whether you like it or not. Even if there are things within the Bible that we don't understand or seem to be impossible, the simple fact that we don't agree or understand does not negate that it is factual.

As Tim explained to Larry, just because we don't know or understand how gravity works does not mean that it is not real. I can declare that for me there is no such thing as gravity. I can refuse to believe in it because I cannot see or touch it. But in spite of my declaration and unbelief, I will continue to walk on the ground and things that I drop will still fall to the ground. My declaration of unbelief does not change truth.

It is the same way with things of God. Your understanding or belief in something does not bring credibility to it. The Bible already has credibility based on God as the author. We cannot honestly say that we believe in God and what He has done to save us, and not believe that He is telling us the truth in the Bible. Picking and choosing what you will and will not believe is a form of idolatry. In essence, you are saying that you know more and have greater wisdom than God who created you.

There is no gray area with God. You are either a believer or not. It's black or white, life or death, Heaven or Hell. He is the Creator and we are His creation. When we forget this, we begin to compare ourselves with God. Comparison with God and equality with Him is what Lucifer desired. This desiring of equality with God is not new, but it is just as dangerous today as it was then. And God will correct us just as harshly if we do not repent of it.

Accepting that the Bible is true is at the foundation of our faith. The Bible isn't simply a series of words on paper written by a number of men. It is a document that not only chronicles the past, but also foretells God's plan for the future. The historical quality of the Bible is amazing. Nowhere else are the formation and development of the Jewish and Christian faiths recorded and explained in such detail. It chronicles happenings and gives specific times and places. Its historical accuracy has been proven time and time again. But still, there are many recorded events that people tend to dismiss as fiction. What they actually end up doing is discrediting the Bible as a whole in their minds.

My wife and I enjoy going out to dinner. When we go to a buffet, I enjoy trying new foods, so I try a little of almost everything. My wife usually sticks with foods she is familiar with. Both approaches are fine when you are at a buffet for dinner. Unfortunately many people approach the Word of God as if it were a buffet. They pick and choose what parts they like and what parts they will believe and refuse the rest, as if to say that they have some sort of above-average knowledge of past happenings. It is a dangerous undertaking!

Not understanding how something in scripture can be true is different than saying that because you don't understand it, it is wrong. There are many mysteries in scripture that scholars who have studied for years cannot fully explain. If God intended you to understand it, He would not have called it a mystery. It is when our pride and arrogance get in the way that we begin to idolize ourselves. When you or your actions state that if it were true, you would understand it, you put yourself and your intellect as the judge of what is true. This is a dangerous place to be. It can start you down a road where you enable yourself to create your own god.

Designing a belief system that is solely based on things that you agree with is pride. God will turn His face from you. He has given us His word so that we would be able to know more about Him and how He works in the world. By forsaking some of His teachings, you are forsaking Him.

It is not easy for an unbeliever to believe that the Bible is completely true. It takes faith to come to that conclusion. Hebrews 11:6 tells us that "...without faith it is impossible to please God, because anyone who comes to Him must first believe that He exists and that He rewards those who earnestly seek Him." It is important to remember that it is not a prerequisite for us to completely *understand* everything in the Bible to *believe* everything that is written there. There are supernatural events that are recorded that no one can completely explain. They are beyond our understanding, requiring us to trust Him.

Let's look at one of the most popular comments about attempting to prove that that the Bible cannot be true: "It was written by men, not God." First, let's agree that the "writers" of the books of the Bible were humans. They actually held the pens that created the words on the scrolls. God Himself did not supernaturally move the pen across the paper without using humans as His tools in this process. But is that what the critics are trying to say? Not usually. What they are usually trying to say is that the men who held the pen came up with the ideas and stories apart from God, and therefore it cannot be called "God's word." The next section about Tim shows how we see and accept this technique of communication every day.

As Tim reached his desk on Wednesday, he noticed a manila envelope waiting for him. In the eight months that he had worked for the firm, he had never once had an envelope waiting on his desk. Usually if someone wanted to give him something, it was in his mailbox down the hall.

What is this? he thought as he put down his briefcase and took the envelope into his hands. He unclasped the back and slid out several pages. There were twenty-three pages stapled together, entitled, "Our Future—Your Part." It was from Wayne, the senior partner. As Tim sat in his chair and began to scan through the memo, he got excited about the direction the company was going and the future he saw for himself with them.

Later while he was at lunch, Sue, one of the secretaries, sat with him. "How is your day going, Sue?" he asked. She looked tired and overworked.

"I'm okay. How about you?"

"I'm doing well. I hope you don't mind me saying, but you look tired today. Are you having a rough day?"

> "Well, actually, yesterday was a rough day. Today I'm just playing catch up. You know the memo you all got this morning? I was the one who put that together for Wayne. He was adamant that everyone had to have it today, so I worked 15 hours yesterday just to get it done. I even hand delivered it last night to everyone's desk so they'd be sure to get it. I really wanted to take today off, but I have too many other things to finish up."

Was the message on everyone's desks from Sue? No. We would all agree that the message was from Wayne, the boss. He used the secretary as his delivery system for his message to his staff. In the same way, the Bible may have been "written" by man's hand, but its message was inspired by God. The author and composer of the message was God, and the delivery system for the message was man. To say that since Sue typed the memo and printed it out for each employee, that it was her message is just as foolish as to say the Bible is written by men, since men wrote the message they heard from God. The author of a work is the one who has the idea for it and expresses it, not necessarily the one who moves the pen on paper. Why did God use a selected number of men to reach others with His message? Why didn't He just impart this knowledge in some supernatural way, apart from human involvement? Nobody knows. He did it in the way He wanted to and for His reason.

If we read the Bible, continually second-guessing the scriptures, it will short-circuit the Spirit's ability to work in our life. When we come to the Bible with the faith that there is a God and He has given us His Word through prophets and scribes, we find that it will change our lives. When we simply put our faith in God and His ability to reveal His desires for us through the written Word, He will honor our faith and speak to us. He will bring healing and restoration to our life as we soak in His message. The choice is, as it always has been, to put our faith in God and His Word or to walk in darkness and never know the joy that He has set before us.

Trust in God and His Word. Read His Word and believe in it, even when you don't understand it. It is not like a regular book that we read and simply gain information from. It is a living thing that actually changes us, shapes us into who we were designed to be as we read it. When we don't fully understand what we read, He will be faithful to bring understanding to us if we are faithful in seeking after Him. He desires that we become more like His Son, Jesus. The best way to do that is to read the Bible, having our mind transformed and renewed. Then we will be able to follow His teachings and commands, and show the world what God can do for them (Rom. 12:2).

Begin your journey through this amazing book that God has given us. He has left it for us as a guide; and if we don't use it, we will be missing one of the most amazing gifts we could imagine. We all have busy lives. We all run to and fro, trying to fit everything into the time we have been given. But let's not let that stop us from getting involved in reading God's Word on a regular basis. That doesn't mean once every three years. It means every day.

Get a guide to aide you in reading through the Bible in a year and follow the program every year. I personally enjoy using the "book at a time" reading plan from *www.discipleshipjournal.com*. It walks you through the Bible in a year, but you don't skip around from book to book, you begin reading a book and continue through it until the end, gaining a wonderful perspective on the author's viewpoint and complete context. You won't be lured into taking things out of context, confusing issues and forming false doctrines. You will simply read the inspired Word of God and gain insight and understanding throughout the year.

I recommend using a guide like this because of the overwhelming size of the Bible. You can commit to reading the Bible in a year without a guide; but without some way of breaking it into “bite-sized” pieces, it can be an overwhelming task, resulting in frustration and giving up. The “Discipleship Journal” has been a great tool for me for breaking apart the Bible into manageable pieces, for tracking my progress, and for inspiring me to continue reading. I pray that your encounter with God’s Word will truly be a life-changing experience that will grow you into who God desires you to be.

Reflection

What truths in the Bible are hardest for you to believe and put into practice?

1.
2.
3.

What scriptures have you taken out of context to give you freedom from obeying Jesus' commands?

1.
2.
3.

Why is it important for you to trust that the things in scripture are true?

1.
2.
3.

CHAPTER 10
VISION—CAN YOU SEE WHERE YOU'RE GOING?

"Well, the next life has to be better than this one!" complained Pete, a middle-aged lawyer who had just gone through a messy divorce.

"What do you mean?" Tim asked.

"Well, the way I look at it, I've paid my dues. I've been through hell the last three years. It can't get any worse than this! It has to be better on the other side." He smiled and looked at his watch. "Well, kid," he continued, "I've gotta get back to work. I'll see you later." As Pete stirred his coffee and walked away, Tim had an empty feeling in his stomach. Pete was lost, and in denial about his part in bringing about this situation. And all of Tim's attempts at getting him to talk about God had failed.

Pete was a good guy. He had been through so much in his life. He rarely was able to see his little boy, even though he had visitation rights every week. His married life with his ex-wife had been miserable, and his divorce was worse. He had been put through so much hurt and torment that he had lost his trust in people and considered true love and friendship a fairy tale. It was his choices in the past that had shaped his present, but in his eyes it was the result of life simply being a hard, dark place where you have to look after yourself and trust nobody. And he definitely couldn't

> see that it was his choice that would determine his eternal future!

How many "Petes" do you know? How many times have you heard a similar story from someone who has been through a tough time in their life and through that time, has lost their faith in God and His power? Unfortunately, it is a common situation in our world. Thankfully, that unbelieving spirit can be broken and faith in God can be built.

We are living in a world that we have created by our choices. For the most part, our present is a direct result of our past. We are brought up in a culture that talks about having it now, living life to fulfill your desires, seizing the day, getting what you want, and never thinking about the future consequences of these actions. This philosophy doesn't work in the long run, either in the physical world or the spiritual.

Our reactions to situations in our life that we cannot control are our own responsibility. We cannot determine where we are born, how we are raised or what we are taught at a young age. We are somewhat dependent on the people around us to be good influences in our life, to love and care for us, and to teach us how to live life. For many, the experience of early life is far from a fairy tale! We grow up in a home that doesn't express love, but rather hate and fighting. We go to school and are taught that we cannot pray because it might offend someone, and that our existence is merely accidental. We are rewarded for learning philosophies from around the world, but are not allowed to open the Bible.

No wonder when we are older and going through trials in life, we don't know what to do. We reach for things to comfort us momentarily that are tools of destruction, like alcohol and drugs. Why would we reach out for God's help when we have been taught that He is a story that only uneducated people believe in? Why would we seek help from others when we are taught that only the strong are meant to survive? Our thoughts are greatly dictated by what we learn and by our sinful nature. That is why we need to read God's Word to soak in truth that will help us in our time of need.

We are focused so much on temporary goals and desires that we often miss the big picture of life. We have the mindset that we can do what we want, and if for some crazy reason there are consequences to our actions, we can fix them later. We have the idea that we will be living here on this planet for at least eighty years, so there is plenty of time to take care of things like consequences, making amends with loved ones, finding out about life after death. We are almost in denial about death when we are young. We think, "Why should I think about my eternal future? I have things to do!" We miss the fact that the "things" we have to do would be different and more fulfilling if we settled the eternal question first.

Our focus in life is usually now, sometimes tomorrow, but very rarely later. It is no wonder why, when presented with the Gospel, people often don't even take time to let the reality of their own death sink in. They hear the Word of God and close off their minds to the possibility of needing Him, or even of Him existing at all. The only time we ever seem to universally think about our own death is at the funerals of others.

Maybe this is why James said, "Grieve, mourn and wail. Change your laughter to mourning and your joy to gloom. Humble yourselves before the Lord and He will lift you up" (James 4:9-10).

He knew that it is better to be presented with our own mortality through another's death and to come to the reality of our own mortality than to be in denial of our short time here and to miss an eternity with God. People need to realize that time really does fly and very soon they will be presented with the reality of death. If people could understand how short their life is, they would consider eternity more seriously. The truth is that physical death is knocking on the door of our life from the moment we are born!

Often when young people tragically die in automobile accidents, we hear comments like "They had their whole life ahead of them." What they really mean is that we think that they should still be here because they were young. None of us are guaranteed a certain number of days. The reality is that we will live every second that God desires us to live, not a second more. His plan for them, while it doesn't make sense to us, was to live a shorter time on this planet. None of us know how long we are to be here. But even if we were here for one hundred years, it would be a blink of an eye compared to life in eternity. God doesn't work in terms of time. His plans are beyond our time—in eternity.

If we could start to grasp the idea of eternity, we would have no problem with investing our short life into God's work. We would be able to see that our reward for a short amount of effort would pay huge dividends. But often we are blinded, seeing only the present age and unable to see eternity. This makes us want to hold onto things and to not freely give of ourselves.

We need to embrace that God's plan is for us to live with Him, eternally. When we find this truth, we can let go of the lies we have believed as a child. We can let go of the idea of having no purpose as accidental beings. We can let go of the teaching that promotes a self-centered generation, and can grasp the truth that we are here for a divine purpose—a destiny.

If we were all given a glimpse into our eternal future, we would see that our time here needs to be used more wisely. If we would see the incredible joy that awaits us as a free gift of God, we would have the strength to press on and go through the trials of life. We would understand that they are God's tools to shape us. Some would be horrified to see the eternal frustration and agony that awaits them, being separated from God and anything that satisfies their souls. It would be enough to wake them up to a dark reality and to make a change in where they stand with the Creator.

If somehow we could have a window into the future, our present would be changed. Fortunately, we were given just that! Through God's Word, we have been given a glimpse into the future. We have been given the gift of God's eternal perspective. He desires to share with us what awaits those who call out to Him, those who recognize His presence and are willing to ask for His gift. He wants nothing more than to have you experience good things and be with Him.

He is faithful in pursuing us, but also is courteous enough to let us make our own decisions. He desires us to *want* to love and be with Him. If He simply created us and forced us to love Him, what kind of love would that be? It wouldn't be love at all!

He already loves you completely. He always has. All He desires is true love from you. Take Him at His word and trust Him with your life. He cares more about your welfare and happiness than you do. He desires to give you good gifts and to bless you. He has shared His plan in His Word. Read it and accept the gift and transformation of your life that He desires for you. You can trust Him.

Reflection

What tends to be your focus in life right now?

1.
2.
3.

If you knew exactly how many days you had left on earth, how would your life be different?

1.
2.
3.

How can you live more in light of eternity on a daily basis?

1.
2.
3.

CHAPTER 11
RUNNING CORPSES?

Tim's career was beginning to soar. The office had picked up several new clients, and his boss had trusted him to take on more responsibility. Leadership had tested his abilities several times, and every time he came through with flying colors. Their confidence in him was growing; and because of that, they were giving him more work to handle.

What used to be a regular, nine-to-five job was rapidly growing into a sixty-hour workweek. His free time was beginning to slip away and with it, his quiet time with God. He really wanted to spend time reading scripture and praying, but couldn't wake up early enough to do it. He never quite had enough room during the day; and when he got home, he was too tired to think about anything that was meaningful.

In addition, his relationship with Pastor Steve began to slip. He didn't make regular visits any longer; and when he did finally have time, he thought he would be too imposing. So he rarely called or stopped by.

One morning when Tim was rushing to the office, Pastor Steve caught his eye, waved, and motioned for him to come over and chat. Pastor Steve was changing the little wooden sign in front of the church door. It reminded Tim of how he met Pastor

Steve and of the feeling of fulfillment and joy that he used to have. He wanted that back in his life.

He waved to Pastor Steve, but kept walking, not wanting to be asked why he had missed the last three Sundays at church. Pastor Steve sighed, smiled back and kept working on the sign. Pastor Steve walked into the church and began to prepare the sermon for this week. He was disappointed that Tim hadn't stopped and wondered if somehow he could have done more for him.

About an hour later there was a small, faint knock on the door. Tim walked in, shuffled into Pastor Steve's office with his head hanging slightly lower than normal.

"Tim!" Pastor Steve exclaimed. "Shouldn't you be at work?"

"No. I should be here," Tim replied. "I should have been here a lot more than I have been lately. That's the problem."

"Well, I'm glad that you're here now!" Pastor Steve poured Tim a cup of coffee. "So, tell me, Tim, what's going on?"

"Well, Pastor Steve, I have been so busy at work. It's been great for my career, but everything else seems like it's dying. I'm sorry that I didn't stop and say hi this morning. I needed to get to the office and didn't think I would get there on time if I stopped."

Looking at his watch, Pastor Steve asked, "It's not lunch time yet. Are you on break?"

"No. I told my boss I don't feel well and I need to go home, rest, and come back tomorrow rested and ready to go. He agreed." Tim chuckled and added, "So here I am, trying to get all better."

Pastor Steve smiled. "I'm glad you're here, Tim. I was thinking about you this morning. Then

I saw you walk by. I wanted to see how you were doing. It seems like it's been so long. I am preparing my sermon for Sunday. Can I share part of it with you?"

"Sure," responded Tim, "but I will definitely be here Sunday. I need to be here. I feel like a part of me is dead. I need to get back to normal."

"It's interesting that you mentioned feeling like that!" Pastor Steve continued. "My sermon is about feeling dead. But it's a good thing sometimes." Tim had a confused look on his face as he sipped the hot coffee. "Let me explain.

"When you think of someone who has died, the image of them running in a marathon doesn't typically come to mind. Usually we think of the relationship we had with them, the things they accomplished during their life and the people that they influenced.

"But strangely enough, a running corpse is one of the pictures that best describes the Christian life. To truly walk with Jesus Christ on a daily basis, we need to die. We need to die to ourselves and allow Him to live through us. If we are unwilling to do this, our walk with Him won't be effective. In fact, it won't be a walk at all. It will be a daily struggle—a tug-of-war so to speak."

"Amen to that!" declared Tim. "I'm living proof."

"Recently while I was reflecting on this, I saw an image of two people going for a walk down a long, tree-lined road on a fall day. The sun was shining, the trees were full of color, and the breeze was blowing gently. One person was the Lord and the other was myself. As we began our journey, we were side by side, almost as one person, having the same destination in mind, enjoying the beauty and splendor that the road had to offer.

"We were close enough to chat, even whisper to each other. We remarked to each other about the beauty that was before us and talked about whatever was on our minds. As we progressed, I began to drift, ever so slightly, from the exact path the Lord was taking. Maybe the rocky, unpaved road was too rough on my bare feet, so I was trying to find a more comfortable path. Maybe the sun was in my eyes and I was seeking a tree-shaded path. Whatever the reason, I began to drift. Not enough to make a difference, I thought, just enough to make it better.

"I wasn't headed in the opposite direction. I didn't take a left turn, or try to hide from the Lord. I just simply wasn't any longer at His side. We continued to walk further down the road, and suddenly I realized that even though I had not really strayed from Him, something was different. I missed something.

"We had stopped talking as we had been. We were no longer close enough to whisper and laugh together. I was only a few steps away, but it felt as if it were miles. I was now leading my own way and I was taking steps where He was not. We were close, but no longer on the exact same path. We would end up at the same location, most likely, but He took one path and I took another. Suddenly we weren't really taking a walk together, but separate walks, just near each other."

"That's exactly how it's been for me lately," Tim inserted.

"Tim, have you ever gone alone to a park and walked along a trail or bike path, or maybe along the beach in the morning to watch the sunrise before anyone was awake, and realized you were not truly alone, but others were there as well? Maybe someone was walking their dog, or someone was rollerblading past you and you said a quick hello."

"Sure. Probably many times," Tim answered.

"You were technically on the same path, the same road, maybe even having the same destination in mind, but you were walking separately, alone. You weren't walking with them, they just happened to be on the same path. So many times this is what ends up happening to us on our walk with Jesus Christ. We suddenly look up and find out that, even though we have a lot of people on the path with us, we are alone, walking out our own course.

"This is a sad state to be in and it can happen quickly, almost without warning. When you began your walk with Christ, I told you to find a group of believers to fellowship with, a church. This is one of the keys to maintaining your walk and growing in your relationship with Christ. It is through the church—His body—that you will be strengthened and encouraged to fight the good fight. But to do that, you need not only to attend a church, but participate in it.

"When the church was formed and ordained by Jesus, it was not His intention that we go for an hour a week to a place, sing some songs and listen to someone talk, then go home. It was a place where believers, members of His body, would come together to learn, strengthen and grow with one another. It was, and still is, the place to go to pour into others' lives and let them pour into ours. We need to be transparent with other believers, at least one or two close friends and mentors, so we will be sure that we are continuing on the journey to which we were called, not miles away from where Jesus desires us to be.

"In 1 Corinthians 15:31, Paul tells us that he dies daily and then goes on and says, '...I mean that[!]....' He knew what it was to have his own desires stripped from him and replaced with the desires that God had for him. Like Paul, we need to be willing to let Jesus keep us on the path He desires us to be on, regardless of what may happen to us physically. Paul lost everything, was thrown in prison, and was beaten for the sake of the Gospel. But during this, he realized that if he continued to walk the path that would fulfill his own desires, he would ultimately be a failure. He would have gained the world he wanted, but lost everything spiritually (Mark 8:36).

"We need to follow the example that Paul left for us. We need to be running corpses. By letting our human will and desires die daily, and following God's will and desire for our lives, we are acting by faith. We are truly offering our bodies as living sacrifices to God (Rom. 12:1), and by doing so, giving God a level of worship that He desires from us. We recognize Jesus as Lord of our lives by not withholding anything from Him and by recognizing that all we have is His to do with as He pleases. We are merely vessels to do His will and to run His race.

"Paul tells us we are all to run our race well. Actually, he tells us that we are to run our race in order to win the prize! We are to be as focused on our walk with Him as an athlete is focused on physical training before entering in the Olympics! Just as athletes will spend years training for a chance to compete in the Olympics, we are to invest our life in Him so that His desire for us will be accomplished before He calls us home. Our life is not our own (1 Cor. 6:19), so we have no right to decide what we are to do with it. Our life was purchased by the blood of Jesus so that He could accomplish His will and purpose through us.

"I encourage you to seek God's will for your life. I encourage you to spend time in quiet reflection and ask Him what He desires from you. What goal has He planned for you to achieve? What prize does He desire you to win for Him?

"After you pray and seek His will, I pray that you will pray for strength to lay down your own goals and desires and to pick up the desires He has for you. I pray that you will die to yourself and will allow Him to refresh your emptiness with Himself. It is the only way that you will be able to accomplish your Kingdom purpose. You can't do it alone. Only He can do it through you, but first He needs you to be a willing vessel.

"I pray that you will have the courage to ask Him what His desire is for you and that you will have the courage to respond with a resounding 'YES!' Be a running corpse, Tim. Run your race well!"

Tim thought about what Pastor Steve had said. It seemed like a great weight had once again been lifted from him. "Thanks, Pastor Steve. I really needed to hear that. I have been walking alone way too long. It's time to come back and start again."

Reflection

What races are you running right now?

1.

2.

3.

Are you submitted to God in such a way that you will follow Him no matter what?

1.

2.

3.

What do you sense God calling you to do that you might not want to do right now?

What steps can you take to grow into acceptance of His will for your life?

1.

2.

3.

CHAPTER 12
THANKFUL FOR HARDSHIP?

As Tim walked past Frank's office, he noticed that Frank was not acting like his normal self. He was gripping his forehead with one hand and his coffee mug with the other as he stared into the air. He had a look of anger and frustration on his face that Tim hadn't seen before. For the last several months, Tim and Frank had been developing a close friendship. They had enjoyed some great discussions in the break room while playing cards. They played in the same golf league and spent many evenings at Frank and Jodi's house watching ball games or movies. Frank seemed like a completely different person today. Something was definitely wrong.

"What's up? You look terrible. Are you okay?" Tim asked. Frank lifted his head slowly, let go of his coffee cup and looked over at him, seeming to look right through him in a daze.

"I'm okay," he replied in a sober voice, appearing to be trying to get his emotions under control.

"What's going on?" Tim insisted, as he pulled up a seat next to him.

"I just got off the phone with my brother. My father died this morning," he said, trying to hold back the emotions that welled up within him. "I guess it was a heart attack."

"I'm so sorry," Tim replied, trying to think of something comforting but realizing that nothing he said would be able to really help.

"He wasn't even old. He wasn't sick. He's just gone. I never even got to say goodbye," Frank continued. "How can this happen to people?" He looked at Tim as if expecting a brilliant, soothing answer that would somehow make things better.

"I'm so sorry," Tim choked out, still wondering what he could possibly say or how he could possibly help his friend. He had never personally gone through something like this and really didn't know what to say or do. The question "Can I pray for you?" finally found its way out of his mouth.

"Pray?" Frank looked at him like he had four heads. "What good will that do? He's not coming back."

Tim could see the desperation and anger in Frank's glare. "I meant for you...and for Jodi...for strength to get through this."

"Well, I definitely need something. I just want to know where God was when he collapsed. Why didn't He do something about it then? Couldn't He see that Dad needed help?" Frank sobbed.

Losing a job or seeing loved ones ravaged by a sickness are probably not the first things that come to mind when you read that we are to be thankful for everything (Eph 5:19-20). In the fifth chapter of his letter to the Ephesians, Paul is teaching the people how to live a godly life. In 1 Thessalonians 5:18, Paul again instructs us to be thankful. This time he admonishes us to be thankful *in* all situations. He encourages us to give God thanks *for* everything and *in* all situations. But how can we do that? Didn't Paul realize that there will be times of hardship in our lives? Didn't he realize that there will be times of pain, when we feel that God has abandoned us?

I assure you he was more aware of hardship than you or I will ever be. Paul had spent years wearing chains in prison for his faith in Jesus. He lost everything he had and saw his friends imprisoned and martyred for their faith. He was aware of what pain and suffering are, but still encourages us to be faithful to God in the midst of our suffering. He knew that when we lose everything for Jesus, we actually will gain more. Sometimes we need to be thankful out of simple obedience to God's commands, just because He is God.

It is very easy to praise God for the blessings that He bestows on us, or the prayers that He so graciously answers. But even as we praise Him for these things, He is still to be praised for the trials that He allows in our lives. I am reminded of Job, when his wife came to him after he had suffered and lost so much. She encouraged him to curse God and die. She was trying to get Job to come to terms with the suffering that he was facing by using human logic. She knew that Job was a righteous man, and therefore God had no "right" to do the things He had done. But Job realized that God remains the same, regardless of what circumstances we are going through. He remains a loving, righteous, Holy God. He has not and will not change. Job showed that he was truly a righteous, God-loving man by the response he gave to the trials in his life.

It is so easy to get caught up in thinking like Job's wife. When things are going well for us, it is easy to act like righteous people and praise God, giving Him the credit. But our true self will be revealed when trials surround our life. What we do then will expose our true thoughts and feelings toward God.

Stressful situations are a part of life. They are like a fork in the road for almost everyone. People can choose to follow their instincts, which say that God has forsaken them at that point, or they can choose to believe His words about never leaving us. In times like these, in a split second, many will decide to trust God and others will decide to turn from Him and believe the lie that He has forgotten them.

What you believe about God in general will shape the decision that you make at this crucial time in your life. Is He trustworthy? Is He truly a good God? Does He actually care about me, personally? Where is He when stressful things happen? These questions are ones that people throughout the ages have been asking when trials come into their lives. So, what are the answers?

I want to look at the last question. "Where was God when …… happened?" This is one of the most common and life-altering questions asked during times of trial and adversity. To really get through a time of hardship, you need to find the answer to this question. If you don't, it will haunt you and possibly destroy your faith in God. Not finding the answer will either inhibit you from ever starting a relationship with Him or will build a spiritual wall around you so that you will no longer be able to experience and trust God in the future. So, what is the answer? Where was He? Where is He now? Why didn't He help?

To find the answer, first I want you to look once again at the story of Job and get some principles to apply to your life. Job experienced more hardship than most of us ever will. He not only lost his belongings and his business but his family, and finally his health. God allowed him to be stripped of everything in the world, down to an empty shell of a man so He could refill his empty shell with everything, both physically and spiritually.

Job had more reason to doubt and not trust that God is a good God than anyone I ever hope to meet.

Job remained true to his understanding of who God is and what God's character says about Him. He was able to continue to trust and praise God in spite of the circumstances around him. He worshipped God by acting out his faith in God's goodness. He truly believed that God had his best interest in mind when He allowed these things to come into his life, regardless of whether or not he understood why. He understood that even if he didn't understand why God would allow these things, that God is the Creator and has every right to do anything that He desires.

Job had no way of understanding that God had allowed these things into his life to test him and to prove to Satan that he truly was a righteous, God-fearing and God-loving man. Job had no way of knowing that God would use these events and his reactions to them to further His kingdom for generations to come. Job could have easily looked at his situation in a worldly, selfish way, blaming God for the torment he underwent and losing faith that God is truly who He says He is.

We need to have an eternal perspective on events in our lives. If we could look at the circumstances that seem grim to us through the eyes of God, I assure you that we would not see them as a dead end, but as part of a wonderful unfolding plan that is accomplishing great purposes throughout the world for ages to come. Our perspective of our circumstances needs to change if we are ever to be thankful for everything.

When Paul was encouraging us to continually give thanks, he was not living in an ideal situation or one that he would have desired or planned for. He was in Rome as a prisoner in chains for preaching the Gospel. He understood hardship, but he never let the hardships cloud his view of his calling and purpose. Like Paul, we need to have the mind of Christ when we come against the hardships of life.

When we ask God to reveal to us what His purpose is in a particular situation, He will be faithful and allow us to see how this temporary setback will have lasting change for the better. When we are focused on the eternal purposes of God, our trials are put into perspective. We can see that though they hurt and are painful for a time, in the long run, God will use them to help us grow into the person He desires us to be. We will see that without Him bringing painful experiences into our lives, we would never be able to grow as He desires us to grow. That doesn't mean the trials don't hurt while we are going through them, but we can rely on God's grace to get us through.

Many times people say something like, "I have this situation going on, pray that Satan will be cast out," or "Pray for me that God will change this situation I am facing." While at times these can be good prayers, the reality is that many times God uses these hard situations to shape us and grow us. Not every "bad" situation in our life is from Satan. And God will not change every situation that we consider "bad." So many times we are trying to cast Satan out, when in reality it is God trying to get our attention so we will repent and turn to Him. Like Job, He uses "bad" things in our life to test, shape, grow and refine us into the image of Christ.

So, where is God when things happen in our lives? He is standing next to us, holding us up and strengthening us through the circumstances. For this reason, we can truly be thankful when we are confronted with a challenging situation or hardship. It shows that God cares enough about us to put things in our lives that are designed to change us and grow us. He desires us to be like His Son and will not stop bringing things into our life until we are. And the double blessing is that He doesn't bring these trials, then leave the room and shut the door. He stands with us as we deal with them, strengthening us in the process. He brings the trial and He brings His grace to conquer the trial. It is up to us to take the grace He brings, learn how to use it, and grow through the process of facing trials.

Like Frank, who suddenly lost his father, the next question many people ask is "Why does God do these 'terrible' things and why is He 'unable' to prevent them?" The truth is that He was more than capable of preventing the situation, but He desires you to grow and to learn a specific thing that you would not have learned any other way. What we think was a terrible, malicious act of God is really a way of taking us down a road with Him, experiencing something together with Him, learning how to trust Him in a new way, and coming out the other side in a deeper, more intimate friendship with Him.

If we got what we desired all the time or if God kept everything that we consider "bad" from us, we would miss out on blessings that He has for us. By allowing us to experience trials, He forces us to look to Him and trust Him. When we are faced with difficulty, often we look to God for comfort, direction and help. He helps us to redirect our focus from our troubles back to Him. By doing so, we gain a new perspective on our lives and a new understanding of His grace and love. That is how we can truly praise Him during the hard times in life. It isn't about avoiding hardship or being in denial that we are grieving, but about gaining God's perspective on the hardships He allows.

Reflection

Think back to times in your life where you have grown the most spiritually. List three of these times below. Were they times of blessing or times of trial?

1.

2.

3.

Is your response to hardships normally one of thanksgiving and worship or of frustration? Why do you think that is?

What steps can you take to make thanksgiving and worship your response to every circumstance, even the heartbreaking ones?

1.

2.

3.

CHAPTER 13
SHADES OF SIN

As Tim made his way from his office to the church to meet Pastor Steve for lunch, the conversation with one of his co-workers was racing through his head. Was he really a "closed-minded bigot?" *I think of myself as a pretty open-minded, caring person,* Tim said to himself as he trudged through the snow. *Am I fooling myself?* He turned onto the nicely shoveled sidewalk. *I want to be open to others' ideas, but how can I defend my position without giving the impression that I'm closed minded?* As he waited for Pastor Steve to answer the bell, he continued to process their conversation.

"Hi, Tim! How are you?" asked Pastor Steve with a smile, but when he saw his friend's face, the smile disappeared. "Are you okay? What's wrong?"

"Hi, Pastor Steve." Tim shook the snow off his boots. "I'm not sure if anything is really wrong. But I do want to run something past you."

"Well, come on into my office and have a seat." Pastor Steve poured Tim a cup of coffee and reclined in his desk chair.

"You see, there's this guy at work," Tim began. "He and I had a pretty heated, uh, discussion this morning and it didn't go that well. Now he thinks I'm a bigot, and I'm not really, I don't think."

"What were you two talking about?"

"Well, as you know, I've been trying to start 'God' conversations with people at work—to see where they're at. We were both getting coffee this morning. He knows I'm a believer. I know he's not. So he pointed out the article in the paper about a gay rights rally, something about gay marriage. He wanted to know what I thought about it. I told him that the Bible tells us clearly that homosexuality is a sin and therefore we should not practice it. Well! He went off, telling me that it's a physical thing, that people can't help it, and who am I to judge people. I tried to tell him that I'm not judging them; I'm just telling him what the Bible says. I tried to tell him how God obviously never intended that to happen since He created man and woman to have babies and populate the earth. And if it were a natural thing, other species would have homosexuals in the same proportion that we do.

"So we ended our discussion by him telling me that I'm a closed-minded bigot, and then walking away. I'm not sure what to do. Do I talk to him again or just drop it?"

"Well, you've already had quite the day!" replied Pastor Steve with a look of compassion on his face. "It seems that you have touched on a sore spot for your friend.

"Tim, I want you to make sure you keep a couple of things in mind as you talk to him about this issue. And yes, I think you need to talk to him again and clear this up. First, I believe that the Bible is quite clear on the topic. The first chapter of Romans is quite clear that because of sin, people will leave natural sexual relations for unnatural, sinful ones. It is also written that God's laws are designed to benefit and help us in our lives. God expects believers to obey them as best they can. In Romans, Paul tells us that we should not use grace as a license to sin. We are to adhere to God's will and desire for us.

"He also desires all people to come to know Him. What you have to remember is that before you accepted His gift of salvation, you were responsible for carrying your own sin. Now that you have accepted His salvation, Jesus has taken your sin on Himself. The sin you committed before and the sin you still commit is just that—sin. The Bible says that if you are guilty of breaking a part of the law, you are guilty of breaking the whole law. So, even if you commit what you consider to be a 'small' sin, it still separates you from God. It's all the same in His eyes. It doesn't matter if you steal a pack of gum or murder someone—it's all sin and needs to be forgiven. There is only one place in the Bible that talks about one sin being 'worse' than another. Jesus says that the only sin that will not be forgiven is a sin against the Holy Spirit! Other than that, it's all the same. Don't think that just because you have made one sin 'bigger' in your own mind that God feels the same.

"I suggest you go to your friend and show him the love that God is offering him so that he can enjoy the salvation Jesus paid for him. By loving him, you will share more about God's law than by telling him about how sinful he is acting. Now, you definitely don't want to condone his actions, but love him in spite of his choice."

"That makes a lot of sense," Tim answered. "I guess I was just thinking about it as being a 'worse' sin, but you're right. Sin is sin. I'll have to talk to him when I get back."

"If any one of you is without sin, let him be the first to throw a stone at her" (John 8:7). This is a familiar passage, but does it mean that we should not point out when someone is acting in a sinful manner? The Pharisees brought a woman to Jesus who was caught in adultery and asked Him what should be done with her. According to the Law, she was to be stoned. He made His reply and began to draw in the sand with His finger. I imagine that the men standing around her with stones in hand, ready to throw them at this woman, went through a process of searching out their own hearts. They quickly recalled countless times they had not measured up to the Law of God. How could they, being sinners, condemn a sinner?

Obviously, Jesus wasn't condoning what she had done. The reality is that He was the only one who had a right to pick up a stone and condemn her, but what did He do instead? After everyone had left the area, and Jesus was alone with this woman, He did not condemn her for her actions, but forgave her. Then He commanded her to leave her sinful actions behind. If this is Jesus' response to someone who has knowingly committed a sin, why should our response, as fellow sinners, be any different?

We need to have the heart and attitude of Jesus toward those who are lost and living in a pit of sin. Our responsibility is to offer them the same love that Jesus offered to this woman. We are not to condemn, but to love. We get so caught up in pointing out the sinful behaviors of others that we forget to remember that we ourselves have been saved from the same! We were black as coal with sin and have been washed white through Jesus' blood. Others need to experience what we have experienced. They don't need our judgment.

If we as a church would do a better job of loving people and condemning sin, we would find our churches growing faster and being more fruitful. Sharing God's love and the saving power of the Gospel with someone, bringing them to fellowship, and letting the Spirit convict them and change their heart will make a radical change in the church! Often we try to share the Gospel, explain all the things that they will have to give up or change, then invite them to become part of a fellowship. Would you have been excited to hear about everything you needed to change in your life before you could attend a fellowship?? This method is not based on scripture, nor does it work! Let's get back to preaching the Gospel and loving people. Let the Spirit do His job of convicting hearts and changing lives!

Although we are not in the position to condemn someone for their sin, we also ought not to be condoning their wrongful actions. Again, there is a balance we need to achieve to live out our Christian faith. The balance is not an easy one, but it is necessary to fulfill who we are called to be—His body. We need to witness to the world about our *changed* lives and at the same time love them where they are. We need to remember that the sinful, lost state we were saved from is the same sinful state that they are currently in, whether or not the manifestation of that state is different. We can love people into a relationship with Christ by accepting them as a creation of God, desperately in need of knowing their Creator. If we come across as though we have our act together and that they need to do the same, it will likely scare people into rebellion or lead them to not trust God.

If, because of our attitude and actions, they see God primarily as a God of anger and judgment who is unhappy with their actions and wants them to completely change before coming into His presence, they will turn away. That is not an accurate picture of God to portray. We need to remember that God humbled Himself and came to earth in the likeness of one of His very creatures. If He was willing to do that for us, how much more humble and loving should we be to another who is lost, just as we were lost? Pray that you never lose touch with the place that you were saved from so that you never lose the desire to bring others from that place to God's house!

If we look at the bigger picture, we will see that there is a bigger problem than the "big" issues of today, such as homosexuality, adultery, and divorce. Pride within the church is a problem that extends far beyond them all. Often we will "see" the "big" issues as Satan's plan of attack at weakening our society and trying to force God and His plan out of our world. And this is true, Satan obviously wants God's plan to fail; but he has a bigger agenda that, for the most part, we overlook completely.

Jesus is going to come back for His bride, the church. He desires to have a spotless, blameless bride for Himself. And while we, the church, try to put on a front that we are living this Christian life in a blameless way, we are only fooling ourselves. When we start thinking of ourselves as better than the world around us, we develop an attitude of pride that Satan will use to destroy us. Satan isn't as interested in bringing non-believers into deeper depths of sin as he is in making believers turn one degree off the mark of living sanctified through Jesus' work.

When an openly sinful man comes to know Jesus, it is obvious to him what wrongs he has committed and why he needs the forgiveness that Jesus offers. He repents, asks for forgiveness and receives it. Members of the church need the same heart attitude when dealing with the attitude of pride. But sadly, too often the repentance never comes. The danger of this is that without recognition of sin, there will be no repentance, and without repentance, there will be a break in fellowship with God. Our pride short-circuits the sanctification that God is giving us, and Satan's scheme has begun to work.

Once we have broken fellowship, we experience a loss of His power in our lives. It is not that we have lost our salvation, but His Spirit is not able to work in us to the same extent if we are not pure. God is perfect in every way, holy and pure, and cannot be around anything that is not pure and holy. Without the power of God working through our life, we are useless to God in the army against Satan. We have no strength within ourselves that is useful in fighting a spiritual battle. We desperately need that Spirit to fight the battle for us, through us, and with us. Without it, we let Satan win.

In the physical world, when there have been wars, the aggressor generally doesn't attack every nation just for the sake of attacking, but hones in on those who present a threat to their empire or their plan. Those are the targets of his warfare. The same is true with Satan. If you are not standing in his way, he isn't as worried about you.

So that is Satan's bigger agenda. That is how he works to corrupt the plans of God. He desires us to be distracted. It's as simple as that. He has used this technique from the beginning, even in the Garden of Eden. He got Adam and Eve distracted from the glorious garden they lived in and the relationship with God they enjoyed, and had them focus on an outside, irrelevant item. Once they did that, they fell right into his hands.

Satan has used this technique from the beginning of creation until now. Why? Because it still works. He wants us to ignore, even for a moment, the relationship with God that we enjoy, the sonship that has been purchased for us, and focus us on outside, irrelevant things or issues. Once this happens, he will be able to distract us from our purpose and from the war, making us useless to God's army.

You may be saying, "I *am* focused on God and His plan!" We may try to be. But the moment we let ourselves believe that our sin, which has been forgiven, is less offensive to God or less of an issue than other people's, we have let pride rear its ugly head in our life. We make ourselves out to be better than them in our minds. We are told in Romans 12:3 not to "...think of yourself more highly than you ought, but rather think of yourself with sober judgment...."

Remember your own sinfulness when confronted with the sins of someone else. Do not fall into the trap Satan has spread out for you. Do not become full of pride and arrogance because you did not fall into the sin that others have fallen into. Do not compare yourself with other "worse sinners," but rather to Christ. He is the goal to strive after. His life is the example, the model, the One in whose likeness we are being conformed. When you start comparing yourself to the sinless One, you gain fresh perspective on your salvation and those drowning in a sea of sin—desperately in need of your prayers and help to find the only One to save them—Jesus Christ.

Reflection

What are some sins that you consider “worse” than others?

1.

2.

3.

How do you think Jesus would respond to people who commit these types of sins?

1.

2.

3.

What keeps you from responding that way?

1.

2.

3.

CHAPTER 14
GETTING BACK TO THE BASICS

As Tim stepped off the plane in a small town in western India, a wall of heat met him. During the whole trip there, he thought about his family back in the States. He had never been away from home during the Christmas season before. For that matter, he had never been warm during Christmas! He walked down the ramp, not knowing what to expect from his short stay with Pastor Keith. As he entered the crowded terminal, he spotted Pastor Keith sitting and talking with a small group of people. Pastor Keith waved and stood up to greet him.

"Welcome to India, my friend!" Pastor Keith called as he approached.

"Thank you," Tim replied. "It's great to be here." He smiled at the small group.

"Tim, these are some of my friends from our church," continued Pastor Keith. "We were just talking about you. We are very excited to have you help us with our outreach program."

As Pastor Keith translated greetings back and forth, Tim had an overwhelming sense that he was exactly where he was supposed to be. He couldn't explain it. It was almost eerie. As they walked down the long, crowded hallway to get his bag, he tried his best to communicate with his new friends. He had spent the last several months trying to learn to speak some Tamil for his trip. But he still had so much to learn! The tapes he bought promised that he would be speaking in a matter of weeks, but he could barely remember basic phrases. He silently prayed that while he was here he would be able to communicate with people.

As he found his bags, two of the men with Pastor Keith smiled at him and took his bags. "You don't have to carry them," Tim exclaimed.

"My friend, let them help you. They want to help you while you are here helping us," Pastor Keith responded. Tim smiled at the men and nodded. They seemed so happy to help him. "Tim, we have a busy two weeks ahead of us. We will get something to eat when we get back to the house and go over our plans."

It was a few days before Christmas. Tim expected to see a display of lights, trees and festivities. Instead, what he found would change the direction of his life forever. As they approached the village, Tim noticed the absence of the typical Christmas he was used to. As a matter of fact, it was noticeably absent.

He remembered the years of celebrating Christmas as a child. The decorated trees, stacks of presents adorned with shiny paper, and the food. The food seemed to never end during the holidays! Going from party to party, eating and sharing the season with loved ones and friends—that was Christmas, wasn't it?

As he walked through the small village following Pastor Keith, every eye was on him. He was the center of everyone's focus, but oddly, he didn't feel nervous or afraid. He noticed their joy and hospitality. As he passed people, they would smile at him and wave, as if they were welcoming someone of noble descent. Pastor Keith had been sharing with them for some time now about his brother from the United States who would be coming to help them. They were anxious to have him come, and now that he was here, they were overjoyed. What would he be able to make happen in their town? Tim wondered. What wonderful things would he be able to do there that Pastor Keith had not been able to do without him?

As Pastor Keith led him into his small, brown house at the end of the dirt street, Tim thought, *I hope I can measure up to half of what they expect.* Two men carried Tim's bags into his room and laid them on his bed. They smiled and nodded at Tim, waved to Pastor Keith, and walked out into the crowd that now surrounded the door.

"Tim, I hope you will be comfortable here. You are a blessing, and we are all so thankful that God has loaned you to us."

Tim smiled and replied, "I hope I am able to help you while I'm here. I feel like I'm in over my head."

"That's nonsense! You have everything you need to fulfill God's purpose for you, both here and back home. You are not alone. Always remember that and you will be okay. Now, wash up and I will be back in a while to bring you to dinner. We have prepared a dinner to welcome you."

Over the next several days, Pastor Keith went over his plans with Tim and three elders from their church for what they hoped to accomplish while Tim was there. They desperately desired to build a new church for their community. They were meeting in a dilapidated pavilion in the middle of the town. Pastor Keith's hope was that if they were able to either fix that one or build a new one, they would be able to better reach the surrounding villages. He thought that people would be more willing to come if they knew they would have a spot under the shade of the roof instead of sitting on the grass in the hot sun.

"Pastor Keith, I don't want to step on any toes, but are you sure that the reason they aren't coming is the building? Or is it that they just don't understand why you meet in the first place?" Tim asked.

"Well, Tim, that's a good question. What makes you think that?"

"In the town I'm from," Tim answered, "there are four churches. They all have nice buildings, heat in winter, air conditioning in the summer, lights, sound systems, the works. But the funny thing is that you probably are getting a higher percentage of your town than they are. It's not the building. It's the message. People will come to hear the message of hope and peace that Jesus has, not to sit in a comfortable chair.

"I have to tell you," Tim went on, "that I have never met so many people with such joy and love for Jesus than I have met here in your village. We get so worked up over this holiday back home. It has literally turned from a time to worship and praise God for His salvation into a season of seeing how much we can get. People go into debt trying to buy stuff for each other in the name of Christmas and then think it's crazy when you want to go to church. It has completely lost its meaning along the way. People think that it's all about Santa, but they forget that the original "Santa," or Saint Nicholas, was a Christian missionary! The same is true for Easter. Today, it is just a day to eat a lot of sugar and candy, not about celebrating Christ's resurrection.

"It amazes me that even though the people of your village have none of the stuff that Americans would consider necessities to celebrate Christmas, they are more worshipful and excited about Jesus' birthday that I have ever experienced! It is truly awesome. And that doesn't come from a building. It comes from a love for God inside their hearts. I think what we need to do is stop worrying so much about the building and start sharing with the other towns why we're so happy. Am I crazy or does that make sense to you?"

Pastor Keith and the others sat in silence. Deep down, they had all known the same thing all along, but they had gotten off track. Their original goal was to plant one new church each year in the surrounding areas. What they had accomplished over the past three years was to plant one church and allow it to consume their energy and focus, distracting them from the work God had given them of planting churches.

A tear began to roll down Pastor Keith's cheek. "You're absolutely right. We need to do more preaching of the Gospel to them and stop worrying where they'll sit until they're here. Tim, thank you. God has been showing me lately that we need to do more to reach the other towns, but I was always so focused on our church and getting a building for them that I forgot the basics."

Over the next 10 days Pastor Keith, Tim and the others developed a plan to divide the area into smaller targets and blanket each one with the Gospel. They divided into teams and began to boldly share their faith with people on the streets and in the markets. Each morning Pastor Keith would give them encouragement and send them out in groups of two or three, and each evening they would come back and share what the Lord had done through them. Over the 10 day blitz, they saw over 200 people come to faith and over 75 percent of them commit to coming to Pastor Keith's church for follow-up each week. It was an incredible result for such a small band of warriors. Tim was amazed at how the Lord was working through this small group of faithful servants. His eyes were opened to God's power to change lives.

What about your church? What about you? Have you lost your focus on evangelism and been sidetracked by other things? Have you lost the real meaning of holidays and gotten caught in the trap of our culture? Today, even churches and religious organizations tend to follow their traditions and customs and not focus on God as much as the reflections of God's presence. So many Christians have adopted the practices of the world instead of changing the world with the Gospel.

Take time to evaluate your life and the life of your church family, and see where and how you can once again experience the God of the universe in the way He intended you to know Him, without all of the symbolism and fluff, but as the real, loving Creator and Savior, Jesus Christ. Get back to the basics and rediscover who Jesus is!

"I wish I could stay longer," Tim told Pastor Keith as he packed his bag on his last day. He had developed a friendship with many of the men he worked with and wanted to continue seeing God use him to reach others. "I can't explain it, but I felt so comfortable working with you," Tim added. "It was as if I finally found my destiny."

"I understand," Pastor Keith replied. "You should pray, my friend. Ask God what His plan is for your life. God answers prayer. The real question is, are you willing to answer His call?"

Tim almost fell over at Pastor Keith's reply. Immediately his mind brought him back to the day

> he saw the words on the sign in front of the church, "God answers prayer. Are you willing to answer His call?" He felt himself get hot and cold all at the same time. It was as if God was talking directly to him for a brief moment. He finally was able to mutter, "Yes. He does answer prayer," as he slowly swallowed the lump in his throat.
>
> Tim sat in awe for the 18 hours of travel back home. What did that mean? Does God really want him to quit his job and go into full-time ministry? *That's ridiculous!* he thought. *I have no training, no degree. Besides, who am I to teach anyone?*
>
> As he quietly pondered what this all meant, the idea of leaving his job seemed too strange for him to consider. At the same time, going back to his job and working every day in his office lacked the excitement and fulfillment he had just experienced. *Pastor Steve needs to help me sort this mess out!* he thought.

What about your calling? Have you heard the quiet calling of God on your life, prompting you to leave what's familiar and go into uncharted waters? Have you heard Him, but have been too scared to pursue His direction? Many are in that place right now. I assure you that Peter was in that place when Jesus asked him to step out of the boat and walk with Him on the water. If I were in Peter's position, I would have thought, *He must be crazy!*

You need to remember that the same God who spoke the world into existence and knitted you together in your mother's womb knows what is best for you. He will not leave you and will not lead you down a road that will hurt you. He loves you and wants you to fulfill your destiny—a destiny of discipleship.

Reflection

What things in your life have distracted you from focusing on Jesus Christ as the center of your life?

1.
2.
3.

How can you get back to focusing on Him in your life?

1.
2.
3.

What can you do to keep Him the focus in your life?

1.
2.
3.

CHAPTER 15
WAKING UP A SLEEPING CHURCH

Tim! You're gonna be late for our final! These words rang through Tim's head as he headed down the steps of the little white church. He remembered how his friend Jon had been diligent all semester long in making sure he was awake for his class, especially when there was a test!

What would I have done without him? Tim thought. So many times he would stay up late and sleep in, missing either the beginning of the class or the whole thing altogether. Without Jon he would have missed several tests and would have been repeating classes right now instead of beginning his career.

Pastor Steve's message ran through Tim's mind over and over as he thought about Jon. *I haven't talked to him in over a year,* he thought. *How is it that people in our lives who do so much for us for a time seem to vanish into the background afterwards? And who have I been there for like that?* Pastor Steve had been talking that morning about Christians' responsibility to reach others with the Gospel in their places of business, circle of friends, families, etc. and how Americans generally don't even take time to do the little things for people anymore, let alone the life-changing things.

"Think about how thankful you are for that person in your life that helped you in a small way," Pastor Steve had said. "How much more thankful do you think someone would be if you shared with them God's plan for eternity?"

Tim began to think about Jon and remembered that he thought that everyone would go to Heaven. As he put it, "Hell doesn't fit into God's plan for us because He loves people. We all end up in Heaven, regardless of what we believe in." Tim began to realize that sharing the Gospel isn't just a thing we "ought" to do, but rather it is the way we can be partners with God in spreading His love. *I have to get in contact with Jon and talk to him!* he thought.

Tim met Jon for lunch the following Tuesday. It amazed him that it had already been so long since they last got together. He had never told his friend about his faith in Christ. As they talked, Jon shared about the parties he had been to, the girl he was dating and the new car he just leased. Tim listened attentively, but kept thinking about his friend's eternal destination.

"What about you?" Jon finally asked. "What have you been up to? Have you been to any good parties lately?"

Tim swallowed hard. *What is he going to think?* Tim wondered as he prepared to tell his best friend about his faith. "Well, I have been busy." Tim began. "But I have to tell you something. I'm not the same Tim that you knew back in school. I'm really not into the party scene anymore."

"Okay," responded Jon as he leaned forward, interested in what his friend was about to say.

"A while ago, I met someone," Tim continued.

"A girl?" asked Jon.

"No. Not a girl," Tim chuckled.

"Actually he's a pastor. I got talking to him one day and he explained things to me in a way I've never heard them explained before. I found out that Jesus is a real person. He's not just some guy from two thousand years ago. He is God. Let me show you something." Tim added as he pulled out a booklet that explained the Gospel message. He began to tell his friend about sin, separation from God and eternal condemnation. He continued to explain that Jesus is God's only provision for us and that we need to accept Him as our Lord to have eternal life.

Tim looked up to find a tear rolling down Jon's cheek.

"I know," Jon replied.

"What do you mean?" asked Tim, confused.

"I mean I know. I've known for years." Jon paused to hold back the tears. "I grew up in a Christian family. Both my parents are believers. My two sisters are, too. I just couldn't do it." After a pause he continued. "After my parents divorced, I said 'good-bye' to God. I didn't want anything to do with Him. I blamed Him for the hurt. I know it was wrong, but I just did it. I figured that I'm a pretty decent person. My relatives are all 'church' people. I don't really have anything to worry about, you know? I do good things for people. I figure that it's Karma. I will get good things back."

Tim didn't know what to say. He sat silently as his friend pondered what he had shared.

After about a minute, Jon finally looked up at him, smiled and said, "I would love to pray that prayer with you, Tim."

It is more dangerous to think that you are going to Heaven than to know that you are not. People who have made a decision that they are not going to follow Christ are sure that, if His claims are true, they will receive judgment and punishment and are willing to take that chance. The result of their decision is completely their doing and they know that. They are counting on the fact that His claims are not true. They are counting on their belief that their wisdom is true and the Bible is false.

It is much more sad to see someone who thinks they are following Him but in reality are following a dangerous mix of Christianity and New Age, which removes Jesus from the throne. They are not interested in hearing about salvation from sin because they think they already have it. In reality, what they have is a masterminded plan of Satan to lead people away from the one true God.

Since the beginning, Satan has used the Word of God against us so that we will not truly follow Him. He is not unaware of God's Word or His plans. As you will remember, he once was living in the direct company of God as an angel—actually the smartest and most beautiful angel God ever created. Since his betrayal, he has been able to gently twist the Word of God into slight deviations that have led many astray.

What many people fail to understand is that Satan's desire is NOT that we would turn from God and worship him. He is only interested in having us deviate from our intended purpose—to bring glory to God and worship Him alone. In doing so, we will be ripped away from our fellowship with God and because of our imperfection, be deserving of God's judgment.

When Jesus was being tempted in the desert, after 40 days of fasting and praying, Satan asked Him to bow down before him and worship him. But we, in most cases, will never experience a direct request from Satan to worship him. He is usually much more subtle, but the end result remains the same. When he led Adam and Eve to stray from God's promises, he mentioned nothing about his own glory. All he did was manipulate God's promises and His Word so that they slightly deviated from it. From that action of deviation, they were cast from God's prepared place for them, the garden, into a harsh world that would need their own labor to bring forth food.

Satan has not changed his strategy over the centuries. He never needed to. Satan's objective isn't necessarily for us to outwardly worship him and bring others with us. All he needs to do is convince us that the laws and promises of God in the Bible aren't 100% true and he has us! We do not need to profess faith in Satan, but rather, to not profess faith in Jesus Christ as Lord and Savior, and Satan has won.

Jesus told us that He is "...the Way, the Truth and the Life. No one comes to the Father except through [Him]" (John 14:6). With this in mind, we need to realize that the ideas and teachings of the world in which we live are a cesspool of warped Bible interpretations comprised by Satan to mislead us from the truth, as he has been doing proficiently for centuries. We have consistently warped the commands of God into what we want to hear instead of obeying the Creator.

Most "Christian" cults do not create a list of rules and laws to live by that directly contradict the scripture. Satan uses the founders of such cults to wrap the Word of God in disguise and twist it slightly to make their followers believe that they *are* following God's laws.

In America, a country of 250 million people that has 170 million people who profess to be non-believers, we see a tremendous number of misled people who honestly believe that they will be saved. They believe they have found a way to reach God. The reality is that without Jesus Christ as Lord and Savior, you are destined to pay the consequences for your sins yourself—in Hell.

"What's wrong?" asked Stan, Tim's boss, as Tim walked into his office. Tim's happy-go-lucky look had melted away to reveal concern.

"Nothing is really wrong," Tim replied. "But I need to talk to you."

Stan had a bewildered look on his face as Tim began to explain that he was leaving his position and going to become a full-time missionary. His passion to reach others with the Gospel and the incredible peace and fulfillment he felt in doing it were guiding his decision. He had been back in the U.S. for two weeks, and every day he felt like he needed to be somewhere else. India, Africa—he wasn't sure where he would end up, but he knew he was supposed to pursue full-time missionary work.

As Tim left Stan's office and walked to Pastor Steve's office, his emotions were racing. He had just turned down the security of his job and was heading into the unknown. Stan thought he was crazy and had made his feelings known.

What did I just do? Am I crazy? Why would anyone quit their job and do this? Tim began to ask himself as he approached the little white church. As he knocked on the door and saw Pastor Steve walking to the door, he was once again overwhelmed with a sense of peace. *Yes! I am doing the right thing. Who cares what Stan thinks!* he told himself. And this time he really meant it.

> A year later, the intense heat met him again as he stepped off the plane in India. This time as he walked through the crowded airport looking for Pastor Keith, it was different. He wasn't there for another two-week trip, but had agreed to stay with Pastor Keith for two years, helping to build the local church and preach the Gospel alongside him. Tim had gone through the basic training his mission agency provided. He still felt limited in knowledge and experience, but it wasn't as much of a concern for him this time. The peace, excitement and joy he felt outweighed his fears and doubts. He was finally following his calling—his destiny. And he knew it!

Countries are starting to send missionaries to America to wake us up. Countries that we have been sending missionaries to for years are being led to send their own people back to the United States. Many missionaries in those countries find it odd, to say the least, that they are being sent to evangelize this nation for Christ. They hear stories about our mega-churches and about the money we invest in missions programs, and can't imagine what they will be able to do when they get here.

What they find is a massive number of people, even Christians, who have fallen asleep on God. They find countless people who no longer believe there is a God at all; swarms of people who believe any way will get you to Heaven; and others, who place their faith in Jesus Christ and then lay back, assured of salvation, wanting nothing to do with reaching out to others.

The foreign missionaries come here wondering why they came, but soon they wonder why they hadn't come earlier. We have fallen asleep as a nation. We have become too comfortable and focused on our own agenda instead of the heart of God.

What about you? Have you heard the voice of God calling you to serve Him in some way but have thought, “I don’t know how to do that” or “I will give to missions, but I can’t go” or “What if I fail?” My friend, these are all valid concerns, but the one fact that covers them all is that if God has called you to do something, He will provide the means to do it. In fact, it won’t be you doing it, but Him doing it *through* you.

Don’t stay in a place of fear and doubt when God calls you to step out in faith. Strive to answer as Samuel did. He heard the voice of God calling him and simply responded, “Speak, for your servant is listening.” He didn’t ask a lot of questions. He understood that if the Creator of the universe asks you to do something, He is capable to manage the details of the task.

God has a specific purpose—a destiny for each person He has created. He tells us in Jeremiah 29:11 “For I know the plans I have for you,” declares the LORD, “plans to prosper you and not to harm you, plans to give you hope and a future.” His plan for you doesn’t have to be a calling into full-time ministry. God doesn’t have two teams of people. There isn’t an “A” team and a “B” team. As Christians, we are all part of the same team—His Body. And we will only be fulfilled when we follow His plan for our lives.

Strive to have the same response that Samuel had when you hear the Lord calling you. Don’t lie sleeping, missing out on the opportunity that God has for you. Wake up! Don’t be like the disciples in the Garden of Gethsemane who fell asleep while Jesus suffered internal agony.

The world is suffering today and needs to hear the message of Jesus Christ. They need a witness to His power, love and grace.

He stands at the door knocking, hoping you will answer and respond with a resounding "Yes." Wake up and respond. Wake up and discover your destiny of discipleship!

Reflection

In what areas of your spiritual life are you somewhat asleep?

1.

2.

3.

What things are you telling yourself or thinking that are not consistent with the Gospel message?

1.

2.

3.

What can you do daily to awaken and renew your walk with Jesus Christ?

1.

2.

3.

About the Author

Eric and his wife Allison are missionaries with Campus Crusade for Christ. They are serving with The JESUS Film Project, a ministry that focuses on bringing the message of the Gospel to people around the world in their own languages.

In Matthew 28:19, Jesus admonishes us to "make disciples of all nations." Campus Crusade for Christ, founded by Dr. Bill and Vonette Bright, has been dedicated to fulfilling this Great Commission for over 50 years. It is Eric and Allison's prayer that their work with The JESUS Film Project in the Discipleship and Church Planting Department is helping to bring that task to completion.

Eric and Allison are working on developing follow-up resources for people around the world who have accepted the Lord from watching The JESUS Film. The Fosters want to see that each of these new believers is given an opportunity to grow in their new faith and become a devoted follower of Jesus Christ.

Campus Crusade for Christ has no central funds for paying salaries and ministry expenses. Like many other mission organizations, Campus Crusade's staff members depend upon the consistent financial support of concerned individuals and churches.

Your partnership with Eric and Allison can make a difference in reaching people for Christ. You can find out more about their ministry and make a financial commitment to their work by visiting their website www.ericandallison.org.

Printed in the United States
60631LVS00002B/62